Who Am I ...... Really?
A Soul's Journey To The Heavens

By
Patty Kenner

PUBLISHED BY: Patty Kenner

Who Am I ...... Really?

Copyright 2012 by Patty Kenner

This book is a true story. Some names may have been altered to protect those unaware participants. The events and experiences are true as they happen through the eyes of the author.

Adult Reading Material

This book is for all those who question their lives and everything about them. My undying love and gratitude to my husband, Ron, who without his steadfast support and belief in me would not have allowed this story to come to fruition. I give thanks for my beautiful children and family who all played designated roles in my life.

Who Am I...... Really?
A Soul's Journey To The Heavens

Introduction

Death is a funny word. Even just mentioning it people become uncomfortable. Why is that? What are we so afraid of? Really, death is merely a process of life. It's not final, it's merely a process. For some it may be short and simple; for others, it may be long and drawn out.

This all began with a few simple dreams and has turned into a several years project. This is my story and may become yours as well. My story is one of hope and one of truth. My wish is that through reading this one may find peace instead of fear and understanding rather than myth and falsehood.

These words will speak differently to each reader. Yet there is something to be found for everyone. This is my journey and yet the journey of all as well. Within these words may you find whatever is needed.

I was always interested in dreams. Through years of journaling and research, I knew a great deal could be learned. Yet just about two years ago my dreams began to change. Through the symbols, they began to point in a different direction. Simply put; they were pointing out that I was at the end of my journey of life on earth. Yet what exactly did that imply? As I said, it's merely a process.

Stick around and you'll see what I mean. Within the process of life, I learned a great deal about myself and those closest to me.

What I hope to accomplish in this endeavor is to provide comfort and peace for others on this same journey. Also, my goal is to remove the fear where possible and replace it with peace and understanding.

For me, I have been given a gift to present to the masses and I am eternally grateful for this opportunity.

Chapter 1

Ever heard of a bucket list? Neither had Patty until she saw the movie <u>Tuesdays With Morrie</u>, staring Jack Lemmon.

Actually, Patty started her own bucket list some time ago. Then she lost it and had to start another one. It's funny how things change along the way. Although thought provoking, how do you really decide what to put on a wish list of things you want to do before you die; *when you know you are dying*?

Then the next question becomes, how do you know you're dying? But wait; a lot of blanks need to be filled in so let's start at the beginning.

How do you reflect on your past and where do you begin? Do you think of what were the happiest events? Do you envision the most tender moments that brought tears to your eyes? Or do you look at what you leave behind? What contribution did you make that will benefit mankind for years to come?

Patty posed that last question to herself many years ago; twenty-six years ago, to be exact. She asked herself, "If I were to die tomorrow, what am I leaving behind that would benefit anyone"?

It was disheartening to say the least and really made her think. Of course, she would be missed by family and friends but that isn't what she is talking about. How did the world profit by anything she had done in her life? That's what she's talking about. This realization started a search that had been festering inside her for a very long time.

So, it began... Patty had always believed there was more to life than what she could see and feel around her. Little did she know what she would encounter in the coming years?

The evolution of her search for truth began with many questions. How well do we really know ourselves? Oh, sure it seems easy to point out what is wrong with someone else, but what about what was going on inside of her? Does anyone ever really even pay attention?

For Patty, it took nearly forty years before she even started to look.

*****

Oh, Patty grew up just like anyone else. She was born and raised in a small town in Pennsylvania, along with her parents and older brother. She left Danville to go to college and there she would met her husband to be. They got married and moved to the big suburbs of Cleveland.

For Patty, it was a tremendous change, going to the big city. They had three wonderful children, two boys and a girl who were involved with all the sports you can imagine, as well as volunteering at the churches and schools.

Patty's husband traveled with his job and was a great provider. They were really two kids who grew up together.

During this time, Patty's mom, Irene, had been living with their family for about the past ten years. Patty's dad had passed away when she was just nine years old.

Irene had her own living quarters but was still a major part of the family. She had always been healthy; in fact, she didn't even have a family doctor. So, when she came down with the flu, Patty just thought she'd get over it. It came as quite a surprise when Irene ended up in the hospital and came home attached to oxygen. She just never recovered from the flu.

Patty became her caretaker and enjoyed the close time they spent together. For the first few weeks, Irene was stable and then Patty noticed some slight changes. They all knew she was dying. The beautiful part is they could talk about it.

One day Patty said to her, "Mom, do you know how sick you really are?"

"I didn't realize it at first, but I do now", Irene replied. "It's okay; I've lived a good life".

Who Am I ...... Really?

Time moved on and Irene slowly started to decline. Patty began to see more changes and felt Irene's body was slowing down.

The next week a momentous change occurred when Irene started to see people in the room and began to communicate with them. One day, after the onset of this, Patty walked into the room and Irene said, "Who are all these people in the room"?

"I can't see them", Patty replied. "Do you know any of them"? Irene quietly said, "No" and kept right on talking to them.

Patty was quite freaked out although she tried not to show it. Over the next couple of days Irene began to see people she did know, old friends and some family members. Somehow this helped Patty feel better, just knowing they weren't all strangers.

Irene had told her she wasn't afraid to die. During one of their many talks, Irene said, "I've never told you this before but long ago I had a near death experience. "What do you mean?" Patty had never heard this before! Irene said, "Well, it happened a long time ago. I was in the hospital with double pneumonia. I was hovering over my body looking down at it. Two doctors were in the room and I could hear every word that was said. They were arguing over whether to give me a massive dose of penicillin. One said it would kill me; the other said without it I would die. Then I saw this beautiful white light and moved toward it. All I felt was total peace and love. The next thing I knew I was back in my body. I've never told anyone else about it except Jane, (who was her best friend)".

Hearing this Patty was speechless. She also realized that her mom had just shared probably the most intimate experience of her life. Patty had just been given an extraordinary gift!

As Irene continued to converse with these people in the room, Patty asked, "Have you seen Dad yet"? "No, but they told me that he's here".

The next morning Patty went in to check on her. Suddenly, Irene said, "Oh! Your father's here!" Her face lit up like nothing Patty had ever seen before. Irene reached her arms out wide to embrace him and said, "Come here you big lug and give me a hug and a kiss!" Patty, feeling like an intruder, said, "Do you want me to come back later"? "Oh yes, please", Irene replied. There was no doubt whatsoever in Patty's mind that her father was there in the room with her mom.

Throughout the day Patty would look in and check on her whenever she walked past her room. Irene was always talking and animating with someone Patty couldn't see.

Later when she walked in, Irene looked at her, clasped her hands together in joy and said, "Oh, I've just been to the most wonderful party with your father!" The expression and delight on her face was astonishing! Then she giggled like a little girl and said, "Oh, I wish I could tell you everything but they tell me I can't."

Later that afternoon, Patty was sitting in their family room on the couch watching television with her daughter. She looked down on the bottom shelf of the end table and saw the bible. A few days before she had asked Irene, "What's your favorite bible verse?" Immediately, Irene said, "Oh, John...In my house there are many rooms and I go to prepare a place for you..."

As Irene looked down at the bible, she wondered exactly what number that verse was in John. So, she reached down and picked up the bible. She opened it to John and began to read the verse, "In my house there are many rooms". Just at that very moment she heard her mom take two loud deep gasping breaths. Patty and her daughter ran into her room. Patty grabbed her hand. Irene took one more breath and passed on from this early world.

Immediately all the tears flowed like a waterfall. Patty and her daughter hugged each other sobbing. It wasn't till later that Patty thought about the exact moment her mom had left. It was precisely the same moment Patty was reading Irene's favorite bible passage. She had just experienced an extremely powerful moment.

The loss Patty felt was a void like nothing she had ever faced. Then she thought about what a special gift she had been given. She was able to fully share and watch as her mom made her transition. There was sadness and joy all in the same breath. Patty was so grateful to have had this opportunity.

During the time her mom was sick, Patty happened to see part of the Today Show on television. The segment was about two hospice nurses who had written a book called *Final Gifts*. The book consisted of experiences from their patients as they went through the dying process. Patty managed to get hold of the book and read it cover to cover. There was so much valuable information in it and she was captivated.

Hospice had been used for a short time to help with her mom and it made such an impression on her that Patty later became a hospice volunteer. Hospice gave her so much support; she wanted to pay it forward and help others. Patty was learning more about the meaning of life than she ever knew existed.

*****

One day Patty was running some errands and came across a gift shop in her area. She decided to go inside and check it out. The store was filled with shelves of pottery, specialized soaps, candles and many other handmade items from various crafters. Off to one side was a small sign. It said, "Psychic Readings". There was a young woman with dark hair sitting behind the table. Another woman, a client, sat in front of her. As the psychic talked to her, she was drawing a picture.

"What is this all about?" Patty wondered. Curiosity got the best of her so when the woman stood up to leave, Patty wandered over and sat down. She had no idea what to expect.

The psychic explained that she had the ability to see and connect with people who had died. As she began to give Patty a reading, she proceeded to draw a picture of Patty's great-grandmother. Patty never knew her great-grandmother but her Mom had given her pictures, so she did recognize her. Patty took that picture home and compared it to the one she had. It was a duplicate except the profile was facing the opposite direction. When she held them up to a mirror, the images were identical! Needless to say, it was quite shocking!

The medium told Patty that she taught meditation classes and invited her to attend a class. Patty wasn't sure if she should go or not but found herself showing up the next week.

The meditation class was held in a small room at the back of a metaphysical bookstore. Patty was very nervous when she walked in the door. She looked around and saw about fifteen chairs arranged in a circle. There were people milling about and talking. They seemed friendly and came up to introduce themselves. Everyone sat down and the psychic began a guided imagery.

Patty still felt uneasy and even wondered, "What am I doing here?" Yet, after listening to the imagery and experiencing the calming music along with it, she couldn't believe how relaxed she was and how good it felt! She knew she would keep going back!

At this point Patty really began to take personal inventory. What is the real meaning of her life? What is her true purpose? Better yet, what was she supposed to do with this life? One thing for sure, Patty knew she had to find out!

The meditations continued to relax her, while even taking some stress out of her everyday life. She began to see and feel a difference. Everyone around her couldn't help but notice the change as well.

Change is usually scary yet for the first time in her life Patty began to feel good inside. It wasn't just self-esteem; it's something that went far deeper.

No one else seemed to understand her search; it just wasn't possible unless you were doing the same thing. Her family knew something was different, that she was different, but they didn't understand it.

It's sometimes said that often you must lose everything in order to gain everything. That's pretty much what happened to Patty. After going through the divorce, she had to begin all over again. It wasn't easy. It was difficult for everyone involved. All she could hope for is that someday the kids would understand.

Each time Patty meditated the better she felt and the more she learned. It was like being a sponge trying to absorb a lake full of water. She just couldn't get enough!

Along with all she was learning, Patty also discovered there was a place in Indiana that offered spiritual classes on assorted topics that held her interest. After a short period of time, she began going there to broaden her experiences even more. The sponge just grew bigger and so did the lake!

*****

Journaling her dreams gave Patty a new area to explore and she began to discover that what occurred in her life was a story told through her dreams. Everyday brought a new awareness. Most dreams come from our subconscious but boy what we learn from them is like a book of revelation. One thing about the subconscious, since dreams are told in symbols, it can be difficult to ignore them. When we utilize the symbols, it helps to allow our egos to step out of the way.

Picture a part of you that greatly enjoys telling you what to do and making it seem quite glamorous at the same time. Now picture that part going off in the corner and having a seat. That's what symbols do to get the ego to sit down and give us truth as well!

Symbols are a universal language that has been used for a very long time by scientists, mathematicians and many others. While our egos may believe a dream has one meaning; the symbol may tell us it means something completely different. Besides, it's a great deal of fun! Often these dreams speak more truth than we are ready to hear.

While Patty was attending classes, she went to a medium on campus for a reading. This medium also connected with those people who have passed on to spirit world. She still didn't know what to expect. She sat down and after saying a prayer, the medium said, "I have a man named Steve here". Patty was completely blown away! Steve is actually her father. It is not his real name, but the nickname her mom had called him her entire life. The reading continued and Steve suggested Patty read the book *The Blue Island*. He said it would help explain some of his experiences during his passing. Patty was totally dumbfounded by all this. She really didn't know what to think.

The book was out of print but Patty managed to get a copy from a used book store. Channeled from the spirit world, the book describes the sinking of the Titanic and the experiences of the passengers and crew as they went through the dying process. It described their entry into spirit world, what it entailed and offered quite an education. Patty felt as if she had opened a whole new door to something from another world. The more she learned, the more questions that surfaced.

Chapter 2

Patty continued her studies and along the way met a wonderful man, Ron, who was on the same path of discovery. They became good friends and later did some work together. To Patty, Ron was like a beacon of bright light and a shining star all rolled into one. Not only did she feel she found a best friend, but so much more. He held the same principles, morals, dreams and inspirations as she did.

They became partners, married and together began a whole new chapter in life. Or perhaps I should say a whole book!

Their relentless searching lead them to put complete faith in the universe and spiritual realms. In doing that they came to understand that we all create our lives through our choices and actions. What follows is the result from those choices.

Each soul's journey is all about learning from what we experience. Actually, it is through the most difficult experiences where we grow and mature the most. Life is all about soul maturity and development. Every day presents us with new opportunities. What we chose yesterday may not be the same choice we'd make today. Often it takes hindsight to grasp a lesson we need to learn.

*****

Through all this Patty found that the universe has the best plan for each soul in each lifetime. If she would just go along with it and try not to interfere; life turns out far better than she could ever believe. Some days she does quite well at staying out of the way; other days she somehow manages to muck things up. Of course, that usually only happens when she thinks she knows better! At least she is always learning!

You might compare it to listening to your parents while growing up. Sometimes you want to listen and other times you it's as if you're deaf and don't hear anything! Here's the thing about it; no matter what happens you always know there will be another opportunity!

New experiences and new adventures seemed to fill their lives. They both loved to travel and found themselves doing a great deal of it. Ron, this wonderful man, taught her so much! She knows the universe brought him into her life to help answer her questions. They have been together twenty years and she is so grateful for the time and the love they share.

Patty really learned the meaning of unconditional love and being loved just way you are without having to change for anyone else. She is so loved, honored and respected just for being herself, not for being what anyone else wanted her to be.

Along the way Patty also discovered the idea that someone could have previous lives. This gave her a whole new avenue to explore. She devoured many books on the subject and then she got to experience one of her own past lives. At first, she was very skeptical; in fact, she wondered if it was real or if it would even work. Yet once she experienced the past life; she could no longer ignore it, because she relived it!

Eventually, Patty decided to complete her studies in past life regression and became certified to teach others as well as continue her own experiences. Life continued to evolve.

Here is a brief example of one of many past lives Patty experienced. One night she woke up and went to change positions. As she rolled over, she went into a past life.

"I see myself as a male Indian and part of a tribe. (The theme in this past life happens to be about male strength and its importance, at least to him). In this life, I am unable to express my real feelings; I feel that if I do, it would be a weakness. So, I keep everything inside while trying to portray superior male strength on the outside. I have a wife who cares for me, cooks for me and loves me very much. I love her also, but can't express it. In fact, I would do anything to show her and express it if I could keep my male strength. That is more important to me. When this life ends, I am outside my body looking down on the scene. All the members of the tribe come to show their love and support. As I look into their eyes, I can see their emotions and feel their love. Only in this very moment do I see just how wrong I have been. All this time I kept my feelings inside thinking it showed male strength. I realize that the strength was actually in being able to show and express true feelings. That is what the tribe did and it created a bond among them. Here I was working so hard to keep everyone outside. I thought I was strong when it was really the tribe, through expressing themselves, that possessed the greatest strength. The bond among them came as a result."

*****

Following this experience, Patty realized there was a strong link to her current life. Throughout this life, she has always had difficulty expressing her feelings. For a long time, she knew only how to be passive aggressive. Her way of expressing was to feel the anger inside and suppress it, or to burst into tears. She sure couldn't calmly and honestly communicate. Quite a big lesson for this life!

*****

One of the best parts of Patty and Ron's life is the constant interaction with the spirit world. Patty's dad was always very special to Patty. Although he passed over fifty years ago, her dad has become a very frequent visitor. He acts as a guide of sorts for Patty and has saved her from herself many times. He would keep both of them on the right track. Patty would chuckle sometimes when she thought that even from over in spirit world, "I'll still listen to my dad!"

Ron had to get used to his father-in-law hanging around and having an input. Patty couldn't help but laugh when he'd roll his eyes and say, "Your dad's here again!" She knew he was only kidding and she loved it! It was considered a wonderful gift. This same gift is available to everyone on the planet; they just aren't aware of it.

People always seem to want confirmation that loved ones who pass on to spirit world are really alive and well. The first question they usually ask is, "Are they okay?" We can all find out for ourselves. Everyone has the ability inside them; it's just a matter of tapping into it.

The more Patty learned, the more questions she had and the more involved she became. Both the dreams and meditations were having a strong impact on her life. Every morning she and Ron would journal their dreams, work out the symbols and then share them with each other. What they learned is astonishing! Whenever their egos would try to interfere; they always had each other to circumvent it.

With each meditation, Patty opened up more to the world of spirit and the communication that came as the result. Even her intuition became more acute. Often, she didn't always understand the meaning; sometimes she wouldn't even begin to grasp it for months or years to come.

Still, Patty remembered Irene had always listened to her intuition. In fact, one day when Patty was about sixteen, they were shopping on the main street of their small hometown. As they walked down the street, Irene suddenly stopped dead in her tracks. "Mom, what's wrong", Patty asked? "Your grandmother just died", she replied. They hurried home and sure enough, they soon received a phone call that Patty's grandmother, who lived in Canada, had died. Was this intuition or a premonition?

*****

About the time Patty turned 45, she was meditating when her grandmother appeared to her and said, "We're preparing a place here for you." Patty was stunned and said, "How long do I have?" "About nine years", she replied.

Needless to say, when Patty came out of the meditation she was quite upset. If felt as if she was just getting started on a new chapter in her life. Yet the nine years passed and nothing happened. But we'll get to that later.

Patty had to wonder why her grandmother would come and tell her that in about nine years she was going to die. Patty thought, this is one puzzle I can't solve. She also speculated if it was a way to begin the entire process in preparation of what was to come. But back then, she blew it off.

Chapter 3

Remember the saying, "two peas in a pod"? That is a joke Patty and Ron had between them; they were like two peas in a pod.

One day, about the end of January in 2011, Ron said to Patty, "I keep seeing a pea pod but not there is only one pea inside. The other pea has fallen out of the pod". They had no idea what this could possible mean. Were they going in different directions in the work they were doing? That was about the only way they could justify it. Of course, neither one of them wanted to believe anything else! This was the best option. Denial?? Little did they know then just how much everything in their lives would change.

*****

In 2008 Patty had the following dream, "I'm coming out of the depths of the water. I rise up out of the water so my entire body is on top of the water. There is a solid gold door being opened up and kept wide open. It is fixed with a latch like a cord so it cannot close. I step through the door, over the threshold and into a very bright white light. I hear someone say, "Welcome back".

Now Patty realized this is the door to the spiritual realm. Moving up out of the water meant that she came out of her emotions and everything was out in the open. Notice that the door is held open so that it can't be closed. Just keep that in the back of your mind.

This next dream Patty experienced shows the work that we can do while in dream state. "I'm in high school. I can't find my locker. I go through other lockers to find my history book. The locker number is 228. I'm in the hallway and find the locker and the book. I'm so relieved. I wait in the hallway outside the classroom door for the teacher to come get me. Then I can turn in the book and take a shower for graduation. The door opens and he comes over to get me. Then I wake up."

The symbol that I can't find my locker is insecurities about Patty's role in a situation. Hallway is transition and new growth. Number 228 could equal 12 which is the ending of a cycle. Book is moving toward her goals or her book of life. As she does find her locker, she realizes her insecurities. Patty turns in the book; she is finished. The teacher is a guide. Shower is a cleansing and spiritual renewal. The open door shows opportunities and being receptive to a greater enlightenment. See what she means about the ways we can all grow? She is just glad she found the locker and the book. She had no idea what she was graduating from but she was finished.

*****

The patterns of our dreams can also be quite startling. Patty's next dream falls into that category. This is one of the first dreams that began to show that Patty was leaving. It happened on January 31, 2010 when Patty lay down to take a nap. "Ron and I are in the back of a store. We're naked and the doorbell rings. A man comes in with a large bouquet of flowers wrapped in paper. I take them out of the paper; they are in need of water. As we go to leave, a woman with dark hair is by the door. She starts to go outside but left a CD player on the ground and then came back inside. Patty wasn't sure if she was leaving so she said, "Excuse me" and went to go out the door. Patty stepped outside and the woman closed the door behind her. The dark-haired woman said to Ron, "Would you like to get a cup of coffee with me and then go to the movies at 11:00?" Ron replied, "That's my wife and we are going to the movies." Patty stopped at the threshold of the door when she heard that. Then she realized he went ahead and made plans with the dark-haired woman anyway. Patty was very upset that he made plans behind her back. She thought, if he wants to go out with her, then make plans to my face.

Even though in this dream is symbolic, Patty had to ask herself, "Am I dying?" Many times, an old part or aspect of us can die as we grow and mature in development. It really is the death of the old to make way for the new. This is what Patty wanted to believe! She just wasn't ready to consider anything else!

Being naked, means everything is out in the open. The man with the flowers is an angel from spirit world. Closing the door is the door between the two worlds. It is still open but just a little bit. The woman represents who Ron would be with next after Patty is gone.

In the dream Patty is outside which is being in spirit world. She starts to go back in but stops at the threshold. This dream is just a beginning of what is to come. Patty really feels it came in order to help break down her denial.

*****

Dreams are also very creative. Here is another dream which pointed to Patty leaving. It happened months later on, September 8, 2010. "I have to pick out a new bathing suit, either red or white. I pick red. I walk across the river to the bank on the other side. The water is almost up to my neck. When I reach the other side, the bathing suit turns white."

Bathing suit represents an attitude for play, spiritual activity. Red signifies energy; white is truth and purity. I proceed to walk across the river, which is the river of life. I go to the bank on the other side, the world of spirit. This is something I banked on when I reached the other side. The bathing suit turns white, truth and purity. So, this very short dream is one of the earlies times that shows Patty crossing over into spirit world. In the dream, she knew there was no going back.

*****

Inside all of us is what we refer to as our higher self. It is the all-seeing, all knowing part of us and is connected to everything in the universe. The following dream shows Patty's higher self is leaving and letting her know her karma has been completed. "I'm in a room for a meeting with some people from work. One of the presidents was present. There is going to be a party later but first we had work to do. I must do the taxes. Some of the seats are already taken. I go to sit next to Angela and she says, "You can't sit here". "Why not?" I ask. She says, "Because you don't measure up." I grab my things in a huff and say, "Well, excuse me!" I go sit at another table with some other people that are there for the celebration. I realize that I can't work here.

The President is leaving after the celebration so I ask where she is going. She says, "<u>I'm going home.</u>" I say, "Home to Iowa?" She says, "Yes, home to Iowa." Tears fill my eyes and roll down my cheeks. She just looks at me and I say, "<u>I haven't been home in a very long time.</u>" Then I eat some oatmeal and her husband says, "Oh, I'd like some oatmeal." The president knew it was mine and said, "Go ahead and have some and we'll order something in later. She is standing with her back to the doorway facing me. I am facing the doorway, just a few feet from it. I can see outside. I wonder where the secret service men are located. I start to open my mouth to ask and see them outside. She says, "What do you want to know?" "I think I just answered my own question. I was going to ask where the secret service are but I see them." I decide I'll just sit at Angela's table. I go over, sit down and say, "Look, I'm sitting here. I have to do the taxes so you'll just have to deal with it."

*****

This dream points out the "taxes" are something where Patty thinks there is work to do. There really isn't any work for her to do; it's just an unnecessary burden she places on herself. The people seated are parts of the self already completed. Angela is an aspect of Patty that has low self-esteem. Walking away deals with a reaction to someone, reflecting what she really feels inside. "Home is the higher self-leaving after the celebration.

*****

Once you've achieved a certain level of development, the higher self-claims it in twenty-four states. The numerology of Iowa is twenty. This represents the world of spirit and matter; cosmic force. Number twenty is also associated with reincarnation or resurrection. Patty doesn't have to come into the physical body anymore. To "order something in later" is telling the masculine aspect of her to go ahead and eat; there are new possibilities later. The secret service represents service done secretly, unknowing to the conscious part of Patty. Secret is also something you know, but don't want to admit or know. One must be earnest in asking and really want the answer. Angela tries to tell Patty what to do and she ends up telling Angela what to do. Insecurity begets insecurity.

Chapter 4

In November of 2010, Patty had a strange occurrence. Previously she would see what she called sparks of light or orbs. She would see them peripherally, but they would disappear in the blink of an eye. What happened now was something entirely different.

Sometime during the night these beautiful blue lights came in around Patty and started flowing all over her from head to toe. They were the most vibrant color of blue, unlike any color she has ever seen. They appeared one right after another and were about the size of a four-inch square.

In her own mind, Patty put out the thought, "Who are you?" She then heard a deep loud booming voice say, "**I AM THE ALL!**" Of course, that definitely got her attention, but more on that later.

*****

Now, just the day before Ron had a dream where he was signing up for something with the government and he had no insurance. He went to the car and called Patty on the phone. (Phone calls are communication with the other side). As Ron listened to her voice he knew that she was no longer here. She was in heaven. Coincidence? You tell me!

*****

Some time ago, around august of 2008, Patty noticed a change in her meditations. It started with some star beings coming in to do a healing on her back, hips and legs. Then Denny, an old college friend who had died in the 90's appeared for a visit. He said, "I'm glad to see you so happy. You deserve it! I've always loved you."

The next shock came when a biblical figure appeared and said he'd be working with her. She is to start a new project in January 2009. "What kind of project?" Patty asked. He simply put his fingers to his lips. "Ssh, can't tell." She did see herself sitting at her desk working.

Then she saw Ron in the office sitting at his desk. There were black books with gold lettering which he had written. Volumes I, II and III were completed. Volume IV was halfway written and Volume V was yet to be written.

Patty then found she was flying and in the palms of each hand was an open eye. Her third eye was open and she had an open eye on the bottom of each foot. Talk about strange! A healing guide was present helping to release her residual energy from the past.

From there she was taken to spirit world and wearing a white robe. There was one being on each side of her. They went up through the levels so she could see and experience it all.

*****

Patty learned they often needed to have permission and protection to allow her to experience this higher level. Due to the brightness of the light, a protective shield is needed or she would not be able to handle the energy vibration.

Now if you're starting to think she has completely lost her mind, just stay with it because the deeper you go, the more you'll understand. Just try to keep an open mind.

To say that Patty was completely shocked by this meditation would be a gross understatement. The only thought running through her mind was, "<u>What is happening to me?</u>" She knew she had to figure it out. Yet grasping the significance of it all was a completely different road she wasn't ready to travel.

*****

People meditate in a variety of ways. Some may focus on a single object; some chant a mantra, while others use a physical activity such as yoga for meditation. There is no right or wrong way to meditate. It's whatever works best for the individual.

Patty and Ron personally use a meditative CD with music that has you experience an alpha and theta brain wave state. With prayer and the use of the CD they began to discover some of the many levels of existence that are there for everyone.

Along with meditations, they also channel through writing and journaling. The more meditations they experienced; the more open they became to channel the energies from those in the spirit world. So, just because someone passes from this world on to the spirit world; they are very much alive!

Everything revolves around our vibration. The more one meditates, the more that vibration is raised. The higher vibration you maintain, the better you feel! That in itself is incentive to meditate!

*****

Remember how Patty was always very close to her dad? Now she knew it was probably due to many lifetimes shared between them. She felt sure he had to obtain permission, in order to guide her to the extent she had experienced and to be around a great deal of the time. He was always so organized at running things and still never fails to keep them both on track.

The funny thing is the way he comes in is to tickle Patty and Ron under their noses. It feels like someone is tickling your nose with a feather! Sometimes it is enough to drive them nuts! Just kidding. But one thing is for sure; they learned not to ignore him, because that doesn't work anyway. He can be quite persistent!

One of their challenges is to comprehend the way in which the universe operates. Yet they learned the key is to listen and just try to stay out of the way without making assumptions. That in itself can be easier said than done.

*****

One day while living in Illinois, Ron went into meditation and was shown that they were to move to a small town in New Hampshire. Now... who in their right mind would believe something like this, let alone do anything about it? Quietly they were thinking, New Hampshire? You must be nuts!

Here's where the complete trust in the universe comes into play. They decided that the ONLY way they would do anything like that is if they received some kind of sign in the physical world. They couldn't begin to imagine how that would ever happen!

The next day Patty and Ron decided to spend the day at the lake. They got up early and packed a picnic lunch. After hooking up the boat, they took off for the lake. It was a beautiful sunny day with blue skies and a light breeze. They really enjoyed themselves relaxing in the sun and even catching some fish. Just being in nature and around water is food that feeds their souls.

About four o'clock that afternoon it was time to head for home. Again, they discussed the meditation. After arriving home, about an hour later the phone rang. The call was from New Hampshire. It turned out it was from a woman whose daughter had taken one of their workshops in Ohio. She was calling because she wanted them to come to New Hampshire and teach a workshop. Talk about a shock!! But they had asked, and the universe had answered. This sure couldn't be ignored!

So, a few weeks later they drove up to New Hampshire and spent a few days finding a place to live. After that they spent time packing everything up, renting a truck and off they went to New Hampshire. In many ways, it was like starting over or perhaps beginning a new chapter to this book of life they were creating.

*****

Patty and Ron spent five years in New Hampshire teaching students, while at the same time doing all they could to expand themselves. The first year they rented a two-bedroom cabin in a remote area outside one of the small towns. When their lease was up they decided to buy and remodel an old Victorian house. It needed a great deal of work from carpentry, electrical and everything else imaginable. But the price was right.

During this time, they also began studies in Montreal, Canada which meant traveling back and forth every several months. They just wanted to grow in any way possible and Montreal offered them many opportunities to grow and teach. They were also able to complete their bachelor degrees and finish their masters as well.

Their house was made of twenty-one rooms which they completely remodeled. They envisioned their house as a spiritual center and tried everything they could think of to get it off the ground. Sure, they had some students and meditation classes. But it never became what they thought it was supposed to be!

*****

One has often heard, from the bible to Buddhism and every spiritual teaching in between, that in order to gain anything, you must first lose everything. That's pretty much exactly what happened next.

Everything seemed to dissolve. The house became too much financially and nothing they tried really seemed to get the spiritual center off the ground. The more they tried, the more things dried up. In hindsight, they came to realize that the best choice would have been to remodel the house and then sell it. But it proved to be a great learning experience.

This was one of those times Patty and Ron didn't understand exactly what the universe was trying to tell them. Often, they would jump into something because they believed that was what they were supposed to do. Only later would they find out that not only were they wrong; they weren't even close! Somehow, they thought they knew better, yet the universe was telling them otherwise! If they'd only just stayed out of the way...

When things dried up, they decided to move to Florida, mainly because it was a much better climate for Patty's health. Plus, the older they got, the less they could deal with the cold weather, let alone the snow.

Snow in New Hampshire started to arrive in November and often never left till at least April. Couple that with ice storms and wind chills well below zero... you get the idea.

Chapter 5

Putting the house up for sale was rather scary. It took almost nine months to sell. They actually had one offer fall through. Then a second offer gave them hope and things seemed to be moving along.

Patty and Ron had yard sales, sold furniture and did everything they could think of to ease the moving process. Talk about letting go of a lot of stuff! They had shipped their furniture and were ready to close the door on the house. After locking it up they drove down to the real estate office to turn in the keys. Their realtor would act as their power of attorney to sign at the closing. They were on their way or so they thought.

The realtor, Jenny, was walking into the office at the same time they arrived. Patty and Ron took one look at her face and knew something was wrong. Jenny said, "I can't believe I have to tell you this; the deal fell through. I'm so sorry!"

Patty and Ron just looked at each other and laughed. That really shocked Jenny! They said, "Look, our furniture is on its way to Florida and this will all work out. Here are the keys." The look on Jenny's face was one of great relief. She must have expected them to be upset. But they realized this was out of their control; there was nothing they could do. Getting upset would not change anything. Great lesson!

So, they took off for Florida, found an apartment and started a new chapter in their lives in a wonderful climate. Again, their dreams and meditations continued to guide them and provide insight.

*****

Dreams can be rather detailed as previously shown, or they can be quite simple and brief. In November of 2009, Patty had the following dream. "I am shown a martini with two olives and cheese on a stick". Symbolically it means a need for meditation and relaxation to bring balance. It was also a pun for putting on a happy face. This just shows that all you need is a small piece of a dream to give you some insight.

Sometimes the meaning of dreams is minimal, other times even reflective. Then there are always those dreams that are so overpowering you remember them for the rest of your life.

In September of 2010 Patty had one of those dreams that involved her father. Here is her experience. "The doorbell rings. I answer it and Dad is standing there. Even in the dream I know he is dead but I'm so excited to see him in the physical. I give him a big hug. He comes in and sits on the couch and says he wants to talk about some things. He has his legal pad and said, "I'm here to make you realize how special you are to many people both on earth and in the spirit world; your tenure here has been fulfilled with the many lessons you chose to learn. There are a few things left that need to be cleaned up and we will help to be sure all is satisfactory. Once that has happened, you will celebrate. In the time left, make it count. Every thought, every word, every deed, make them count. Have no regrets for anything left unsaid or undone. You have the gift of knowing so use it wisely. That's all for now. I love you Princess!" Even at this point, she still didn't know what he meant about celebrating.

Of course, she ran to tell Ron. Even from the look on his face, she knew he was shocked. "That was no dream", he said, "That experience was real, just as real as you and I sitting here!"

About here is where Patty's denial kicks in and becomes apparent. Notice how subtle the universe can put things, such as 'there are a few things left to clean up and then you will celebrate". Still, Patty couldn't believe she was really leaving, nor did she want to believe it!

These dreams and experiences show the time frame where things began to point to the fact that Patty would be leaving. It also demonstrates her denial!

*****

Remember the book *The Blue Island* that Patty's dad wanted her to read? She had actually read it twice. Still, it came as quite a shock when during one of her meditations in late 2008 she was told she was going to visit the Blue Island. All that she could remember from the experience is that she was shown different layers of various worlds. Each one had a different hue in the color of light that emanated from it. This was one of her first incidents of this kind.

Another first experience happened about a year later. "Patty and Ron are over in spirit world. They go to a training session. It's a place called the Grand Terminal. There are huge white corridors and it's set up like a large wheel with many spokes coming off the center. Patty and Ron each have a ticket and walk up to a glass window. A man behind the counter takes their tickets and stamps them. The stamp says, "Training 10". They enter a nearby room. It is very large and filled with people already seated. Out in the hallway of the terminal they can see it is crowded with people coming and going." The experience comes to an end but later you will hear more about it.

*****

Often these experiences can either be very subtle or rather earth shattering. One of the later occurred in a dream in August of 2009. "Ron and I are together and out of the ethers comes a loud voice that says, "We want to talk to you!" (It sounds like the booming voice of God that you hear in movies!) The room starts to spin around them like a vortex and everything is moving. When it's over, Patty doesn't remember what has been said to them. She asks Ron what happened and told him she couldn't remember. He said, "Don't worry; we're just going to continue doing our work." This was one of those experiences that is so profound you never forget it.

Along with dreams that provide education, Patty learned that the meditations she was experiencing also taught her things she never would have believed possible.

In September of 2009 during a meditation, "A guide came in to teach me about levitation. He instructed me to use both hands to raise myself up and lower myself down to land. I was told to practice which I did. To turn left, I used my left hand. Then I had to practice going in a circle to learn control. I used my right arm to do the same thing. Again, the practice was to learn control. I was like a little kid with a new toy! It was so much fun! Then the next thing I knew, a wizard appears with a purple cloak. He opens up his cloak. There is a white horse there and I climb on his back. We are inside the wizard's cloak. Immediately we go out in the vast universe.

I see a huge city. Here all one must do is think of where you want to go and it happens. There is such a feeling of wholeness and completeness in being here. The next thing I know, I'm with my dad. He has a legal sized book of some kind. We're sitting at this picnic table in spirit world and he's going over some things with me. I ask him to be sure I can bring it all back into a conscious state so I can remember it. He says, "Not just yet princess, but soon."

*****

That same day right after waking up, I wrote the following in my journal. "I am sitting on top of a mountain wearing a white robe. Across from me is a Buddhist priest. I am receiving lessons. A man with a short white beard and white hair comes to me. I ask his name and he says, "Call me David. I am one of the twelve elders. There are many levels here. I am her to provide you the teachings of level 4. Ron is receiving level 7. It is important for you to take it easy the next several weeks. The teachings you both are receiving will continue as scheduled."

, Patty really had no understanding of what was happening to either one of them.

*****

Sometime after receiving certification in past lives, Patty became aware of how much planning took place before we ever come in here as incarnates. Some describe it as a place between lives. It sounds as though it's a separate place. The reality is that there is no separation. Anyhow, Patty decided to explore this area. She had read Newton's book, *Life Between Lives*. He uses hypnosis for clients to experience this in-between state. His teaching was being offered through an organization in Virginia and she decided to attend. The training lasted a week. As part of the process she got to experience this area of existence through the guidance of a therapist using hypnosis.

Patty will never forget what she experienced that day. It is as real to her now as the day it happened. "I am led into a very deep state of hypnosis and taken across the bridge to the other side into spirit world. Dad is waiting for me. We hug each other and he begins to dance with me. One thing I always regretted is that he was not present to dance with me at my wedding. Yet here he is dancing with me! (It is as real as the computer I'm typing on right now!) During this process, my physical body is lying on a bed sobbing like nobody's business. The therapist allowed me to continue to release and spend this time with my dad."

*****

The truth is these tears go back to the nine-year-old little girl who never grieved over her father leaving. What a catharsis! In that moment Patty further realized just how real the spirit world is and that the earth plane is really a dream that we all experience.

"Just as the day my mother died, and Dad came in to help Mom cross over; I have no doubt whatsoever that he was there with me. I also have no doubt about what I experienced when I danced with my father."

*****

Many times, we can receive a spiritual communication and not really understand its meaning. Such an example came in January of 2009 from my dad. "Hi Princess, thanks for letting me in. What a historic day it is there. Times, they are a changing, eh? You and Ron will both be part of that change. There will come a time when each of you will make your own history." Now, how do you begin to explain that one?

We really had no idea what that all meant. Yet it occurred four years ago. Little did I know that I would be sitting here writing this book. Of course, I also didn't have any idea what God had planned. If I had, I probably would have run in the opposite direction.

Who Am I ...... Really?

Someone once said, "If you want to make God laugh, tell him you have a plan!" There is so much truth to that statement. If Patty has learned one thing for sure, it's that any plan God and the universe have is far better than anything she could ever imagine in her wildest dreams!

Chapter 6

In the summer of 2009 Ron and Patty moved back to Florida for the last time. They seemed to have bounced back and forth for several years. In 2008 about a year was spent back in Kentucky. Going through that one winter convinced them to once again head south. Patty had major health problems all her life and the cold weather really compounded things.

So, in late June of that year, they packed up everything they owned and headed south. They were like two little kids off on another adventure. They had found a beautiful place to live and for a while even became beach bums. It is such a terrific experience to play in the water and bake in the sun. We just couldn't get enough.

Then they began to meditate at the beach. The depth that could be reached bordered on comatose. Picture lying in a beach chair listening to the waves gently coming in, feeling the sun and wind on your body. Now you have the picture!

While meditating in 2009, Patty became aware of just how much learning and education is constantly taking place, even if we don't know it. 'There is a guide with white hair that comes in and shows her the church in Gatlinburg, Tennessee where they had gotten married.

"Ron and I are in a class over in spirit world. We finish the class and go up front to get our diplomas. The room is full of people. On the blackboard are all kinds of numbers and equations. Then Ron and I are in a huge circular area taking more classes. There are thousands of people here. It is a new phase of life"

Now we have no clue whatsoever what we accomplished or any idea what it possibly meant!

Yet five days later, she had the following dream. "Ron and I are walking along the beach. Next, we're on horseback riding on the beach. I'm on a white horse. Ron is on a chestnut colored horse. (Symbolically, the beach is the bridge between the physical world and the spiritual world. The fact that I'm on a white horse, deals with the spiritual; the brown horse signifies the earth, material world.)

On the same day Patty had another dream, or perhaps I should say experience. "I'm in the hospital in spirit world. Mom and Dad are in the room, one on either side of the bed. Mom is dressed in her nurses' uniform. Dad says, "Don't worry; everything is going to be okay." Usually when we have a dream that involves someone who is in the spirit world; it really is a true experience that has happened. Since her mom was a nurse when she was here, the fact that she has her nurses' uniform on shows Patty it comes in deal with healing.

What's really interesting is that at this time Patty was having a great deal more health problems. She was having trouble eating, losing weight, severe stomach problems and was in quite a bit of pain. She went to the doctor and they ran about every test imaginable. It actually took nearly six months to diagnose gallbladder problems. Surgery took place in January 2010. In the subsequent first few months she was doing well and able to eat most things. Then after four or five months, she started having similar problems. Returning to the doctor had the result that she would pretty much have to deal with this the rest of her life.

*****

Now, allow me to provide a little more background so you have details. I grew up in a very small town in Pennsylvania. It only had a population of about eight thousand people. For raising a family, it was the ideal situation. Then, after college about twenty some years was spent in Ohio. Growing up I learned from my parents what they learned from their parents being passed down the line. Whether right or wrong, we utilize these traits. They become part of our identity we carry with us throughout this life and other lives. As we grow up we begin to realize that some of these traits we no longer want to carry with us.

Our dreams provide a great avenue for pointing out the areas that should be investigated. It may be aspects of childhood, adulthood or anything in between. This next dream which occurred toward the end of 2010 shows that the old identities from Danville and Cleveland are no longer present.

*****

"I'm on a yellow bus with a bunch of other people. I can't find my melon colored purse. There is a row of purses. I go through them and find a melon purse like mine but when I look inside it there is someone else's license and picture so I put it back. There is a black purse. I go through it and it's empty. The bus is in a field and I decide I'll just get off and walk home." Then I wake up. (Bus has to do with tremendous potential for self-expression. Purses are a whole lot of identity. My subconscious is telling me the identity of the purse isn't mine. The black purse is my identity in Cleveland and Danville and it's empty. My identity there is gone. License is giving myself permission to be happy. The photograph is how I see myself now. The fact that I got off the bus means I'm close to the truth about myself and don't want to face it. In other in the words, I should have stayed on the bus!! More denial!!!)

A few days later Patty had a dream which shows what's keeping her in here. "I'm on vacation and there is a meeting Sunday night at church to plan a festival. On vacation, I see Mr. A and he wants to help. I'm already picking up Mr. B in the same development and Mr. A asks if I will pick him up for the meeting and I say, "Sure." I'm going up cement stairs in my hometown to see a vocal tryout. I'm with a friend Tanya. We get there and a bunch of others are watching. She goes down to the front row and I'm behind her. She sits down and a man comes over for me to buy a ticket. He has a pile of tickets in his hand and pulls one out. I ask how much it is and he says, "$33.00". I say, "No, I don't have $33.00". I get up to leave and start up the stairs. I hear someone in the crowd say, "She tried to sit there before but the seats were full. There was no room." I call to Tanya, 'Tanya, I'm out of here".

I then go up the steps. As I go upstairs I see and old neighbor coming downstairs. She is so surprised and happy to see me and we keep going. After I leave I look at my watch and its 8:30. I know the meeting has already started but I think I'll go anyway. I get there and people are coming out. My brother is with me; most of the people are gone. I ask what the plans are and I'm told we can't have it because there aren't enough people to help and they are $900.00 short."

(Vacations are a time to go within to take a break from beliefs through play and relaxation. Sunday is rest attunement and rejuvenation. The church is the need to awaken and awareness of higher mind. The festival is an initiation, celebration. I'm going upstairs equals new direction in life and I observe healing in expressions of joy and harmony. Tanya in numerology is a 16 which is destruction of the old for rebirth to occur. The ticket is opportunity for new experiences. Thirty-three dollars is being a spiritual master and symbolizes truth. Then I say I don't have thirty-three dollars. I'm not accepting where I'm at, so I leave. As I go upstairs, I see my neighbor who lived across the street when I was growing up. When I leave I look at my watch and its 8:30. That deals with getting on with life and everything depends on timing. 8:30 equals 11 which goes back to the physical realm.

The fact that they are short $900.00 deals with endings of a cycle. The dream points out what is keeping her from going ahead and taking a ticket of balance. I have no changes to make. I can't recall the names from Cleveland so I'm finished there. I just need to release it all.)

Remember it's all about the learning and education of the soul.

*****

The more we utilize our dreams, the more knowledge can be presented. We all dream whether we remember them or not. Many people who say they can't remember their dreams happens because that's exactly what they are telling themselves.

We dream about every ninety minutes throughout the night. The last dream before we wake up is the most important and the longest. It is our lesson dream. It will deliver a box load of information if we pay attention. Dreams provide us with insight on where we stand physically, emotionally, mentally and spiritually.

Equally important are the meditations we experience. The more we meditate, the more insight we receive. Also, the experiences can be profound beyond words. Remember when I said to keep an open mind? Sometimes we can see something in meditation and not understand what it means for months or even years to come.

On February 4, 2010 Patty had one of the strangest meditations. 'I see a white staircase going up. There is a woman who had her left breast removed on one of the stairs. I can see the scar. Her husband is tenderly kissing the scar. Dad is waiting at the top of the stairs wearing a business suit and red tie. I ask where we're going and he says. "To the judges." Then we're in a huge area with a gallery of seats on tiers. I look over and there are twelve beings in what looks like a juror's box.

There is a kind of stage on it and I'm on stage. It is as if I'm on trial. Dad represents me. I'm being asked questions by the twelve beings. I don't know what the questions are but I feel a bit nervous. Dad tells me to relax.

The questions are designed to prepare me for upcoming events. Suddenly, it's over and they tell me I've cleared Level 1 and half of Level 2. Dad is smiling and I'm so relieved.

We leave there are go to a restaurant. A lot of my relatives are there waiting for us. They all clap when we walk inside. Dad says, 'Well, this trial is over." I'm so thankful. I ask what happens from here. Dad says, "There is a great deal I can't tell you. It has to be experienced as it comes." I understand that.

Now we're back in the room with the white marble table and twelve beings. This is a new level of questions. It is explained that they seek to know the soul knowledge that was gained in this incarnation. Then it is compared to what the soul had set up to accomplish in this lifetime.

I have completed my mission and resolved the residual issues and energy that was necessary. It is explained that many souls will decide to accomplish a great deal, almost overload. Then they fall short on the mission. Others may decide to take on a minimal amount to accomplish and they end up completing far more than was necessary. Neither is right or wrong. It is all about learning and growth.

Some souls may choose only to understand emotions such as anger or humility. Therefore, they will experience situations in that regard. It is all about the progressions of the soul. It is only through understanding ourselves that we can understand others.

Next, I am in a smaller room with the recorder at a desk. I sit down and Enoch is beside me. Dad is waiting just outside the door. My time with the recorder is to see how far I've come and to see what is left to do.

He shows me my book. Before it seemed, there was about one fourth of the book left blank. Now it is only about one eighth. It doesn't look like much left. He is very pleased so far. He begins to write in my book. I look down at the page and the ink is gold.

I ask if I may read it and bring it back with me and he says it's not necessary.

Now I'm outside. I look up and see huge rain clouds. I know a storm is coming. I see a tornado forming in Northern Kentucky. It is gaining momentum and traveling south. It comes down the west coast of Florida but stays just out in the ocean, just off the coast. It doesn't come near us, only wind and a few showers. It's all being taken care of and I don't need to worry.

The beach and R & R are needed. There we release energy from the past. It has a great impact.

*****

Patty's next meditation gave insight as to how attached we become to people and things. It occurred in September of 2010. "A white horse came and got me. We rode very fast and jumped in a championship competition where we won a red ribbon. (I have always loved to ride).

A wizard appears and takes me with him. We go through the layers of the universe to the world of plants that actually move. (Yes, there are other worlds). I can hear and see them move.

We continue through the layers of the universe. Then I am given a gift. It is the sword of truth and it is used to cut cords and energy from behind me. I was told I finished Level 4 of the second tier. I was told to ask Ron about it. When they take me there I actually get sick to my stomach and am brought back."

Now Patty really didn't know what she accomplished but something was definitely completed!

(You're probably wondering what is a cord? It's basically an energetic link from one person to another. Think of it as an invisible electric cord plugged from one person to another. We all have cords that link us to other people's energy; especially our families and relatives. The more we are attached to them, the stronger the cord.

The goal is to allow these cords to be severed so that we have no attachments. It's got nothing to do with how much we love these people. It means that we simply allow those people to live their own lives and go through their own lessons without our interference. How often do we try to intervene if we think it will save someone from being hurt? When we do that we do more harm than good. It's their lesson to learn. When we interfere, we keep them from learning that lesson.

If we utilize compassion we can remain detached; if we use empathy; we are sucked into that person's energy and thus a cord can attach.)

*****

Dreams of Patty leaving continued throughout 2010. This next dream involved her mom who is in spirit world. "Mom and I are outside in the driveway. The driveway goes uphill. At the top of the hill is a large cardboard box from a copier. The mailman comes and says, "Sorry, they are coming after you. I said, "What?" She said, "They're coming after you for having a home office." I said, "We don't have a home office." She looks at the box. It was from a copier. I said, "We only pay bills from that room. My husband doesn't get paid from anyone other than his job."

I said to Mom, "What would you do?" She said, "Get a G8 form and fill it out saying you don't have a home office."

(Driveway is the extension of self. It's outside and goes uphill which is the path home to God, making access to outer reality easier. The hill is opportunity for spiritual growth. Box is the games we set up, limits we impose on ourselves. The mailman is a message bearer. Home office is daily work. I said we didn't have one and she looks at the box. I need to start looking at who I'm copying. The copier is ideas multiplying. Paying bills is karmic repayment. The G8 form is another reference to not get involved.)

This dream reinforces things Patty and Ron have been getting about her leaving. The house and driveway are hers over in spirit world. G8 is also the individual karmic liberation.

*****

The on October 14, 2010, the following occurred in a meditation. 'Ron and I are standing on the bank of a river. We are holding each other and kissing, saying goodbye. I must go across the river and he can't come. I go across."

Patty is astonished! This dream certainly speaks for itself. Notice that with each confirmation that is presented; it gets more difficult to deny what is happening!

*****

Just about any time we go to the beach we meditate. Ron and I both found that the energy of the waves and water as well as the sand provide some of the most profound experiences. Often after meditating for an hour, I am barely able to move!

Sometimes when we meditate we are taken so deep that we are unable to bring the experiences back into the conscious state. It can be quite frustrating. You know that something is occurring yet have no conscious recollection.

The next day Patty was meditating and had one of those deep experiences. Then in the blink of an eye, as if a switch was flipped, she became able to receive things. "I am in spirit world in a place of arrivals and departures. I am arriving and it is a very special place. I know I am not departing again. A man with a white beard comes and draws number 77 on my forehead in light." (Number 77 represents the mystic. It is the cosmic evolution going to individual evolution.)

Later in the same meditation, "I am with Mom in spirit world in her garden. The garden is full of roses in every color; these were always her favorite flowers. (Growing up we had rose bushes planted across the front boundary of our property.) We are sitting on a bench talking. Then she goes with Dad and me to the edge of Level 4. She tells me she can go no further. Dad and I continue to Level 5. There is a counter and I hand someone a white ticket. They stamp it Level 5. Next Dad and I are in front of three beings that wear white hoods. This silver metal, which is liquid (the Christ Light), flows into my third eye. I turn into solid blue energy, then purple, then white. When I turn white I start to levitate easily. Through thought, the beings bring me down."

*****

Imagine having to provide a place large enough for each soul that has died. Makes you think, doesn't it? We all have different belief systems and are at various stages of soul development. The fact that Patty's mother had to stay on level four deals with the maturity of her soul level.

Picture this: the planet earth is merely a stage where all souls come to play a certain role in this game of life. Some are villains, some are heroes, or any other possibility one could imagine. It is merely a large school where we keep coming to learn our life lessons! Sound impossible? Just keep listening...

Chapter 7

Growing up Patty always loved horses. There was a stable a few miles from her house. She took lessons and rode whenever possible. Part of the lesson was learning how to care for the horses. One day she hoped to own her own horse. It never happened but she could still dream.

Then in November of 2010, Patty had another profound meditation. "An angel comes to me. She is dressed in pink and takes me over to spirit world where there are actual horse stables. I knew I had a horse over there. The angel asks if I want to ride. Of course, I said, "Yes!" I actually ride in an olympic sized ring. It is so wonderful! I can feel the warmth of the horse under me. As I pet him I feel his soft hair and the coarseness of his mane. It is all so real!

When I finish riding, the angels showed me the inside of a hospital. I find myself then appearing before a council of 7 beings. (Often, we are shown images almost as a flash as if you are watching a movie screen.) There are some legal papers on a table with a gold seal on them.

I see scenes from the moving *Defending Your Life* staring Albert Brooks. (In this movie, he is killed suddenly in a car accident. He then goes before two judges in spirit world where he must defend his life's lessons. Once he does then the judges will decide if he can go on to heaven or if he has to return again to earth.)

There is also some kind of passport I see next. I am able to read part of my obituary in a newspaper. It reads, "Patty Kenner passed away on . . . ", but I can't read the date. The angel tells me to enjoy the time I have left here." It is quite a meditation!

As time continued the meditations seemed to become more intense. One day during a beach meditation, "A white and gold limo comes for me. Dad is seated inside. I am taken to a gold domed building. Dad opens the door to let me out. We walk up about fifteen steps. There are other people on the stairs but they're not allowed to enter the building.

I am then seated on a gold throne and a great deal of energy flows through the top of my head. I see flashes of other people I know are in spirit world.

Master Enoch appears and we go before the Council of 7. There are more legal papers dated July 29, 2010. (Anything that happens here on earth, first happens in the spirit world. "As above, so below".) Just as the meditation ends I see the numbers 44 and 144."

*****

I know these numbers are probably confusing to some people. Actually, our whole world is made up of numbers. It is the matrix, so to speak, but I think that's a whole other book!

Patty didn't know anything about the numbers. She always went to Ron because he has been researching numbers through the bible for years. He knew the meaning of the numbers.

*****

Remember the recorder? He's the one who keeps a record of every event in every soul's life. Well, you're about to hear from him again. It all started with another meditation that Patty had at the beach. "A cable car comes to pick me up. I step on and ride it until it stops in front of a gold sky scraper. I go inside and take the elevator up to the top floor. Two of my favorite former movie actors are there. One tells me that in April I would be seeing more of the big picture.

(You're probably wondering why these famous people would show up in my meditations? I wonder the same thing! I really don't understand why, other than they offer to help from the other side. Also, I have received readings from other mediums where famous people will appear. You'd be amazed that someone you admire or are inspired by will come into your meditation or dream.)

Next, I walk into a room and the recorder is sitting in the corner with my book of life. Most of the pages have writing on them, except the last few pages are blank. On the back cover is written "The End" and he closes the book. A white unicorn shows up and we go out into the universe toward one star. We then become part of the star."

*****

As if these meditations are not strange enough, things were about to change and go in a whole different direction. In the meantime, Patty is just trying to put the pieces together.

Remember those little blue lights that we've mentioned? Well, you're about to understand their significance. But first, on December 21, just as they were waking up, Ron asked, "Did you bring back a dream?" Patty said, "No".

"Why aren't you bringing anything back?' Ron then saw a flash of the number 42. Patty no longer had a need to bring back anything.

The meditations about leaving continued. Patty had an extremely deep meditation on December 22, 2010. "I'm standing on a cul-de-sac at the end of a street. The mail truck pulls up alongside me. The driver hands me a priority envelope made of cardboard. I pull the tear strip to open it. Inside is a legal document with a gold seal on it. It says, "You are scheduled to leave the earth plane of existence on...and she was unable to read the rest; she was not permitted to bring it back." Right now, even denial is in question.

Early the next morning, just as they were waking up, the blue lights surround Patty. They gently begin flowing all over and around her. She decides to go with them and is immediately over in the spirit world in front of her white house. This time one of the lights inside on the left was lit. There are thirteen rooms in the house.

She is instructed to take a tablet with her into meditation. Little did she know what these blue lights were all about or what they would bring. Soon enough, she was going to find out!

*****

Patty never ceases to be amazed at just how the universe can bring a particular lesson in and what it teaches us. On the very last day of 2010, she was in a meditation and experienced a brief past life.

"It is during the 1920's and a black and gold car comes for me. Dad is with me. I know in this life how very much I am loved." (The parallel was this life with mom. After dad died, mom was meant to have a life of her own, to break out of her constraints. Instead she pretty much gave up on life). Then Patty flashes back to a past life with Ron.

"I'm in a huge ballroom dancing. Ron is pursuing me. I love him a great deal. He swears it is only me he loves. I am walking into another room. I see Ron reclined on a settee and three women are swooning all over him. I feel so devastated, humiliated and deeply hurt. I start to break down sobbing in the corner of the room. I have a small derringer gun in the pocket of my dress. I pull it out and kill myself.

Now I am lying in a coffin at the parlor of the funeral home. Ron comes in and the look in his eyes tells me a great deal. He feels responsible for my death. As I hover over my body I know the truth of this life. No one is responsible for my death but me! It is not Ron's fault, the fault is all mine!

Fast forward to this present life. I am lying in a coffin. Ron stands at the bottom, almost as if standing guard yet still feeling the tremendous love we shared. I am hovering over my body where I can access the true lessons in the lifetime.

I understand that my mom was meant to break out of her mold and continue to live after dad died. I was also meant to break out of my mold, to learn to stand on my own two feet. It meant going through a divorce and loving my children while allowing them to lead their own lives. I needed to find my own identity. I must follow my heart, to know love, feel love and safety, in order to be able to complete everything. I am finished.

As I look down at Ron all I feel is the immense love for him and for all we shared together. At the same time I can feel the love of spirit world, a love so magnificent, it makes earthly love seem like a childhood crush!"

Whenever a past life is experienced; we can gain insight merely by asking questions as to what we gained and lost in the experience. We can learn our strengths and weaknesses in that life, what or how we could have done better, and what we have yet to learn, merely by asking. It is all provided to us all we need to do is ask!

*****

Remember the discussion about famous people who show up in dreams and meditations? Patty has always greatly admired one of the former presidents and what he stood for. He was such an inspiration to her. As each New Year comes, people always seem to talk about all the new opportunities that are available. That is just what happened to Patty as she began to meditate.

The date is January 2, 2011 and the meditation begins, "I see my dad and this former president appear. The president said something about this being my final journey. I am dressed in a pilot's uniform. It is a blue skirt and white blouse.

Today is my final exam. I walk down the aisle into the cockpit of the plane. It is a 747 and I am flying for Southwest Airlines (South is spiritual awareness, integrating higher awareness in everyday life. West is exploration, adventure, unconscious or unknown aspect of self). I sit in the captain's seat and the captain, an older man (guide) sits in the other seat. I go through the checklist of everything in the plane and am given clearance for takeoff. I ask, "Where are we going?" "Copenhagen", he says.

I slowly back the plane out of the jet way and head for runway 39er. I am given clearance for takeoff. We start down the runway; I pull back on the throttle and we are airborne. (From this moment, I have no recall. About ten minutes before the meditation tape is due to end, I again have recall).

It is time to land the plane. I ready it for landing and gently bring the plane down to touch on the runway. The brakes are applied and we taxi to the terminal. The captain finishes grading me and says, "Congratulations! You passed with flying colors!" I receive gold wings, gold bars and three gold stars on my lapel."

The profoundness of this experience has stayed with Patty to this day. She has always loved to fly, even as a child. Growing up she wanted to be a stewardess. It probably started when she was just five years old.

Her dad took her on a business trip with him. They flew from Pittsburgh to Minneapolis. It is still a vivid image to her. Back in the 1950's some planes actually had two floors. The downstairs was set up like a conference room. Her dad arranged for her to go into the cockpit to meet the pilot and co-pilot. What an experience for a five year old child!

Is that why she was seeing herself as a pilot? Or could this be a job she would have over in spirit world? Who can say?

Chapter 8

As the new year opened, the changes continued. The following week brought more confirmation for Patty. While meditating, "An angel dressed in a luminescent pink color appeared to me, along with the Anubis. He stayed to my right and the angel was on my left. (I have learned that depending on where we go, often we need others surrounding us to get there.)

They take me to a place filled with a very special energy. It is a forest filled with tall beautiful trees. There is a very lush green grassy area by a large tree with a rock beside it. I sit down and lean against the rock. Soon afterward, all these different angels and nature beings come out around me. I can feel their wings as they flap them near me.

One little sprite comes right up to my face and flaps her little wings. I gently hold out my hand and she lands in my palm. There are also large angels with wings. It is such a special place to see. Their love is so overwhelming!

I never knew such a place existed! What a gift! Once you have an experience like this, you never forget it. Yes, angels are real!

Patty began to receive special channeled teachings from these blue lights. At first it was overwhelming and she felt a great responsibility.

There is so much information being given to Patty, it sometimes makes her head spin. Yet it offers her so much to think about. She began to look forward to these teachings and what was being offered. She wondered when they would come again.

For the most part, they were coming sometime during the night. They would flow around her and ask her to wake up and begin to journal.

Usually this would happen anywhere between 2:00 a.m. and 5:00 a.m. Of course, once she had finished writing, there was no going back to sleep!

For the next week or so things seemed quiet. Yet the dreams kept coming in order for Patty to grow even more. She came to learn that our dreams can also point out to us what we're missing, or what we don't recognize. Patty had such a dream. The date is January 10, 2011. "I am going to a celebration outside. My credit card is in the pocket of my shorts. I go and sit in a car to use my credit card.

Then I'm outside and realize I can't find my credit card. I go back to the car to see if it fell out of my pocket. Inside the car is an oven. I look inside and the credit card is not there."

(Celebration outside represents an initiation. The credit card is getting something you pay for later in life. The dream points out I don't need to incur any more debt. The shorts pocket is a place for hiding, safe keeping. The oven inside the car represents the womb. It is the birth of new ideas, new aspect of self.

In other words, the universe won't let me incur any debt. Part of me that is the new aspect can't incur debt. Because I'm looking for the credit card; I'm not seeing and recognizing this new aspect.)

Then on January 13, 2011, even Patty's meditations began to involve even more. Patty had learned about the White Brotherhood from reading a book about their teachings. These are a group of highly evolved souls whose mission is to educate and bring light to the souls on earth.

On this day, Patty starts to meditate, "There is someone from the White Brotherhood waiting for me. He appears on my right. He says, "Take my hand. I can take you some places you haven't been before."

Then we're standing in front of huge white gates. The gates open by themselves and beyond the gates is a huge white castle. This is so magnificent, unlike anything I've ever seen.

We go inside and I appear before seven beings. I am asked several questions. I am not permitted to bring the answers back to remember.

In the blink of an eye I am paddling a canoe down a river. Ron, some children and many others are on the left bank. I continue past them and there is a place to dock on the right, so I pull in there and get out. There are many people on the right bank, Mom, Dad and many others that I know are in spirit world." All the people on the left bank are those that are on earth; all those on the right bank are those in spirit world.

As if this wasn't enough shock, Patty felt her denial begin to rear its head, yet how could she ignore what had happened?

Her denial shows up the next night in a dream. "I'm going to buy a new car (new identity). I drive to the dealership and arrive at 8:00 when they open. I'm in the passenger seat. No one else is in the car. (God is driving). A car pulls up on my right side. A TV host from a talk show is driving. He works there. It's raining. He gets out of the vehicle.

I look for my umbrella. It's on the floor and I pick it up. I go inside when they turn on the lights. I sit down in a chair and wait for them to open their offices.

A woman comes over with a box of chocolate cookies. She takes a bunch out and puts them on the table. She says, "Mrs. _____" and I say, "No, I'm Mrs. Kenner." She says, "Patty" and I say "Yes". She says, "Please have a cookie. They're really good with coffee."

I thank her and tell her I'm buying a new car and I'm there to find out the price. I eat a cookie while I wait for the offices to open up."

(This dream points out that Patty has a new lifestyle and entrance to a new state of the soul. God is driving since there is no one else in the car. Patty is resisting control. The rain is cleansing in preparation for emotional growth. Lights inside are the wisdom of God, ability to see and understand, Christ light within.

Patty sits in a chair, her position in life. The box of cookies is treating the self and embracing the treat. The woman calls Patty's name but she is not hearing her new identity. She is not Mrs. Kenner, she has a new identity.

The new car is a variety of opportunities for new roles and the price is the value Patty places on herself. See the denial?)

Just three days later, Patty receives more numbers in meditation. "I see Dad. A bright gold light flows through me. There is a tunnel and I go through it. There is a bright blue sphere at the end of it. It turns purple and engulfs me. The numbers 76 and 80 are in front of me. (Patty really doesn't know anything about numbers so she goes to ask Ron. He is all about the numbers and their meanings.

(Seventy-six is the number for termination of individual karma by completion of the cycle of evolution. It is passing from the death of the matter of oneself to the birth of the spiritual. Number eighty is the liberation of all creatures in the cosmos, the nirvana world.)

Next, I see Dad, my grandmother, Ronald Reagan and Ron's dad. Dad gives me this huge beautiful diamond ring. He says it has 72 facets. I also receive a new horse over in spirit world as a result of this new elevation.

Now I am in a hospital in spirit world and all my relatives come to visit. Mom, Dad, Aunt Jean and some friends are all there.

I am sitting up in the hospital bed and am so happy to see everyone. Off to the right is someone from the White Brotherhood. There is also a man with a white beard who is recording everything.

Dad and I get on a silver train going to the place of arrivals. After that we are inside a grocery store shopping. The cart is full of meat and steaks.

From there we are at a barbecue outside Dad's house. The backyard is full of people, relatives and friends. It's a celebration. There is a dessert on the picnic table. It is a white sheet cake with blue and gold decorations. I look at the writing and it says, "Welcome Home Patty".

I hear someone say, "Plan and prepare". After this the bed starts to vibrate and I am gone. Quite a meditation don't you think? Who would ever imagine they have backyard barbecues in spirit world?

But wait, things are just starting to expose even more!

January 19, 2011 during another meditation, "I see Dad. We start going up an escalator. He says, "You were on Level 5 before. You've moved up to Level 6. There are 7 levels and other levels within those seven.

Next, I see a white pickup truck full of garbage bags in the back. We go to a place where the bags are dumped and emptied out. I am told, "Level 6 is the level of spiritual beings that transcend the material earthly world."

I see a purple and blue tunnel. This is another tunnel to an upper elevation. I can hear the most astonishing music and Angelic voices coming out of the tunnel.

I hear someone call out, "Patty, will you come with me?" I ask, "Who are you?" She replies, "I am a higher being Angel of Light." She is dressed in an iridescent pink color. Two other angels appear beside her. They are dressed in blue. Then one changes to a deep purple and the other changes to gold. They each take my arm and we start moving upward.

I ask, "Where are we going?" and hear, "You'll see". I ask, "Will I remember?" and hear, "Yes".

As we move up we are being covered with drops of silvery sparkle energy as if it is raining on us. Only we don't get wet.

I can see a city of energy and lights in the distance. Rainbow colors are everywhere, all iridescent. In front of me is a huge gold throne. They place me on the throne and bow before me. The gold angel is in front with the others on each side. A voice says, "Here is where you'll stay, God's throne within you".

Then they lift me up and bring me back through the layers. I hear them say, "We will come again." These are the Angels of Transition.

Needless to say, all this has quite an impact on Patty and Ron. She has so many feelings and emotions inside. How can she still deny that she is leaving? Some days she does and some days she doesn't.

Ron seems to take it all in and at times is just quiet. All Patty knows in her heart is that all these experiences really happened! For now, that must suffice.

Still, as Patty thinks just about what has happened the last year, or even six months; she can only wonder what's next?

Chapter 9

It appears this week for Patty is quite earth shattering. Although these teachings seem brief, they also speak volumes to anyone willing to listen.

Her meditations on the other hand seemed to have gone to a whole new level. What she is about to experience is almost beyond her comprehension.

On January 22, 2011 Patty began her meditations with her usual prayer. Then her experience starts in the blink of an eye. "I see number 32. Enoch comes for me and there are twelve White Brotherhood with him. They are dressed in white robes with blue and gold down the front. They each carry a staff and as they surround me, I am enveloped by their energy.

We cross the Red Sea. The sea parts so we can cross it.

A winged being appears and asks me to go with him. He wraps his wings around me. We go out into the universe and are drawn to one star, Cyrus, the dog star.

After that I go before seven beings dressed in blue, gold and white. The recorder is also there. I am asked questions. When it is finished, a gold liquid energy comes in through my crown chakra and flows through me.

I am levitated from there. I am being taught how to manifest by thought, travel by thought, everything by thought.

Next, I am shown a place in nature that is in complete balance. I again see friends and relatives there as well.

A deep purple robe is placed around me. The three angels return. They take me to a place and show me a glimpse of the lower realms, all from a distance. It is much like earth because that is the level of thought of the inhabitants.

I am taken back to the level where I belong. The colors are so iridescent like nothing on earth. Everything is alive. I ask, "What do I need to do?" The answer is, "Live each day through the eyes of a child." I see a ticket with the number 4.17 on it.

Now I am in Dad's office. There are some documents on his desk. They all have a gold seal and "Completed" is stamped in them. My time left is for the opportunities to tie up loose ends.

I can see the recorder writing in my book. Only about one fourth of the pages are left, three-fourths are completed. The rest is destiny to play out.

Now I feel really sick to my stomach. I am told I must adjust to the level of energy awareness. Before me there is a huge open eye. I go into it and turn so I can see through it. The angels bring me back."

*****

(Crossing the Red Sea is leaving this world. The number on the ticket, 4.17; four is the natural world, 17 is the nature of the soul. Number 32 is the whole plan of everything in here. The purple robe is the soul level. Either I am taught how to manifest due to personal growth or it's something we all do at night.)

*****

The expansion of the knowledge that is offered gives Patty and Ron a great deal of food for thought and discussion. They both are quite astounded at the information being presented. Couple that with the continuous dreams and they realize everything seems to have a new dimension. The complexity of it all still is difficult to grasp.

For Patty, sometimes she sits in amazement at what is coming through just in her dreams and meditations. She has been searching for a long time as to the meaning of life. Here she is finding out a whole lot more than she could ever imagine.

Her questions are being answered plus she is being given part of the teachings of the entire universe! What is next?

*****

Patty's next meditation occurred on January 25, 2011. It is even more shocking. "I am in a white wedding dress. Two angels in pink are with me. One is on either side of me. Everything around me is gold.

I look up and see a huge dome. There is a gold and silver sphere hovering over my head. We're walking down the aisle of what looks like a cathedral. At the end of the aisle is a gold throne.

We all kneel before the throne and I am placed on it. I hear the music of angels. I look down and see the floor. It is iridescent in color and moving as if it were liquid. To my left is an eagle, to my right is a ram's head. In front of me is a gold cross suspended in the air. The center of the cross is the joining of physical man and spirit.

We get up from the throne. They take me by the arms and we rise up. We move up through the layers. It goes from thick and dense to light and bright.

I look down as we're moving and see lights like sparks. These are the lights I know from past incarnations. We rise through a blue layer and then to a deep purple layer. As the energy surrounds me I feel it penetrating me. What a wonderful feeling!

I ask where we are and the angels say, "Your new kingdom, what you have earned." I see many souls waiting for me and I can feel their love.

There is a beautiful fountain in front of me. It gives off energy, colors and sounds like music. They tell me to feel the water. I reach my hand in and touch it. It feels amazing yet I don't get wet!

All is by thought and I'm learning and practicing. It is easy to think of objects but my thought in travel is not yet smooth. They tell me it will come. For now, they must help me to balance as we travel.

There is someone I must meet with but it is not time yet.

Mom comes dressed in her nurses' uniform. She is so proud to be here. She has earned it.

Next, I'm in a hospital with an IV hocked up. It is to regenerate the soul and remove imbalances. Many are happy to see me. I can hear their thoughts.

There is an old man with a white beard and glasses. I don't know him. Others float by, look and smile at me.

Now the angels take me to the edge of a tunnel. They say goodbye. I am to go into the tunnel. They will see me again. I enter the tunnel and come out by a white gate. I go through the gate. On the other side are two guides I know. They say I am in a level of transition."

There are seven levels of transition. I am on Level 5. I have been to levels six and seven but only for a short while. For now, I remain on Level 5. The rest will come later.

After that I'm in a sweat lodge lying on a bearskin rug. There is a medicine man who is working on me. I am out of my body hovering over it. As he finishes, I re-enter my body."

*****

Patty is still amazed at the realization that one second of meditation you're in one place interacting and in a blink of an eye you're somewhere else doing something completely different. That takes getting used to!

Each day for her seems to be even more profound and surprising. The next meditation she has involves going to the processing terminal. It occurred the next day on January 26, 2011. The dates are provided so a time frame of growth and experiences can be followed.

*****

"Dad is waiting for me and gives me a big hug. We're in a picnic area with beautiful green grass and picnic tables. Many of my relatives and Ron's are there to see me. His dad comes up and hugs me. "You're so good for my son", he said.

The energy here feels very different but I can't explain it. There are large buildings. The sky is the color of the rainbow and gold.

I hear Dad say, "Next we're going to the processing terminal. This is all so you'll recognize it later." It's a huge building and is reddish-brown in color. It is explained that the color inside is far different. The outside is reddish-brown to help balance the energy of those souls entering from dense places like earth.

Many souls have been through a lingering illness which is draining. If the color of this place was too high in vibration, they couldn't handle it. It helps ease the transition for those who need it.

I'm not entering the inside, only seeing the outside.

From here dad says, we go to a rejuvenation center, known as a hospital to me. In a blink, we are there.

Mom is working and wearing her nurses' uniform. I see some souls asleep and others who are up and moving around. The souls that are asleep have an energy vibration so fragile you can feel it.

Now we go along the countryside. Many souls wave as we pass by. There are structures and buildings but most are moving energy structures. Beautiful flowers in all colors are everywhere. I see Master Enoch ahead waiting for me and Dad says it's time for a meeting.

I find myself standing in front of a large white marble table. There are twelve beings seated behind the table. I am being asked questions again. I see a figure from the bible.

Next, I am taken to a place where there are many babies. These are some from abortions and also those souls who changed their minds in utero and were either stillborn, or died shortly after birth. Special care is taken to rejuvenate these souls.

I am being assured that Ron will be well taken care of after I leave. He is so special to many. I ask, "When am I leaving?" I don't receive an answer. I do not wish to cause Ron any difficulty caring for me... then I drift off. I am unable to bring the rest back."

Chapter 10

The month of January isn't even over and it seemed things are escalating. The events leave Patty spellbound. Her meditation on January 27th would provide more information than she could envision!

"I see Dad waiting at the top of an escalator. We greet each other with a hug. I ask where we're going. He says, "It's a surprise."

We travel quickly and I see the picnic area as we pass by. When we stop, it is a place so magical I feel like Dorothy in the Land of Oz. It's difficult to explain. The energy feels so incredibly magnificent it is as if it is filling my whole being. Dad says, "This is your first taste of living in spirit world and how it feels." It truly is indescribable! After our allotted time here, we must leave.

I see a former president and Dad says, "He'd like a word with you." I am honored. He is sitting in a chair and offers me one. He says, "I am glad for this moment. You are very special to many here. You both sell yourselves short.

What you seem to forget is that you have helped many people in your travels. You seem to minimize that. Many of those in which you planted seeds have gone on to mature on their own.

You were only meant to plant the seed. That is all we wanted. It's all about the growth of the self! You are both learning that. You now realize its importance. Please ask Ron for a minute of his time in writing. I do need to speak with him. Thank you my dear, good day."

As I leave he waves goodbye. We begin moving again. There are White Brotherhood beings that surround us as we travel.

It is being explained to me that everything is being orchestrated. There are other things they wish me to be familiar with. Ron and I have reached a level of soul comprehension. It is a merging of unconditional love for each other that has merged with the Divine. This is very special to experience. The merging part is seeing through the veil. I see the number 36. The bed starts to vibrate, and emerald green color flows over me and I'm gone."

*****

As if that experience was not astonishing enough, sometime during the night, Patty heard a loud voice say, "Book!" Then later as if in a dream she saw a column with fiction/non-fiction. Just before she woke up she heard a doorbell ring. (Doorbell sounds or phones ringing are the universe's way of getting our attention).

Patty couldn't help but wonder what all this is about. Is she supposed to write a book? Does this explain why she is receiving all this information? She wonders if maybe for the first time, things are beginning to come together and make some sense? Could she be right?

She continues to learn and transcribe what is being brought to her. The month of January isn't yet over and still there is more to come. There were only a few short days left yet Patty is finding that each meditation provides more information and is deeper and more profound that the previous one.

Her meditation on January 29th, 2011 was one of those. "I see Dad and Enoch waiting for me. I ask where we're going and hear, "to the River of Life." (The River of Life is merely an exit point for those souls leaving the earth plane. It flows for all and must be crossed by all.) They also show me some individual residence places of those I know in spirit world.

I am at Ron's aunt's house. She makes us come tea and serves it in pretty flowered china cups. It tastes unlike anything I've experienced. It definitely takes some getting used to.

\

She is so proud of Ron's studies and helps when she can. She shows me number 99 and then number 69. She says we are just beginning to understand the dynamics of it all. The yard is full of different colored iris, her favorite flower. They are so beautiful!

Once again, I can see the river of life. There are souls that are going across. Then a gap ... I feel I'm not to remember the rest."

*****

Patty still finds all this information overwhelming and difficult to grasp. Yet the experiences are so real, they cannot be denied. The next meditation is even more enlightening!

It occurs on January 30, 2011 and the first fifteen minutes there is a gap ... "A doctor I had on earth years ago comes to me. He tells me not to worry about anything.

Then I'm moving in travel and wearing a glistening gold robe. I find myself at the base of a huge white building. There are a lot of steps to climb to get to the front door. I go up the steps and am waiting outside for someone to show up.

Enoch shows up and then Dad. I ask, "What place is this?" They say it is the Hall of Learning. All knowledge is stored here.

We go inside. It reminds me a bit of a library. I am here to learn how it works. There is a kind of desk with a chair and they ask me to sit down. A strange looking lamp hangs over the table. They tell me to think of something in which you seek information.

I think, "What past life connection is there to the people in my present life?" Immediately the information is displayed on the desk top so I can read it. There is even a diagram much like the Kabbalah Tree of Life. It shows the past life connections with people and the year of the past life.

Any information can be gained here. I think of "colors' and immediately a chart presents itself with shades of colors on earth and another column of those colors in spirit world. Amazing!

Time to leave here. I see my horse and am asked if I'd like to ride. We take off through the countryside and into the woods. It's so beautiful and I feel so free. We cross a stream and stop just to listen to the sounds of nature. Now, I'm back at the horse barn where I feed him two carrots.

Dad wants to talk. We're at the picnic area and sit at a table. Dad and Enoch are across from me. I see three former presidents at another table. Another well-known figure pops in and thanks me for giving a message to Ron.

I ask Enoch if I may ask some questions and he says "Yes". I ask for a time frame of events. He says, "It's undecided as of now." It's important I take stock of what is going on physically and emotionally. They continue to work on both of us to prepare us. It is quite a long process. I ask what I need to do. I am to keep documenting and writing what transpires. Just keep going within and searching my heart. It knows from my soul just what needs to be done and when to do it.

The pain in my legs is connected to what is going on with everything else. It is part of the process. There will come a time when all that will be realized.

Document what you feel physically and what's going on. It will help the whole process. It is all about timing which you will understand later."

*****

For Patty, again she is astonished at all the information that is being presented. Only one last day left in January and still more came.

"As soon as I begin to meditate, the balls of my feet are tingling. I start to count myself down and am told to go up. There is a white staircase going up. I get to the top. There is a long aisle with military guards in dress uniform lining each side of the aisle. They raise their gold swords and the swords meet in the center as I start down the aisle.

At the end of the aisle is Dad. I ask what our agenda is and they say, "Visiting".

First, we are going to the Sacred Gardens. I ask what this is and hear, "You'll see". We start moving through colors. In a blink, I am surround by a deep purple mist. When it clears there is a setting so beautiful it takes my breath away.

Every flower in every color is present. The aroma is intoxicating. I see many souls walking around. When they leave here they are closer to a perfect balance. There are souls who work in this area and help them. The feeling of perfect balance is amazing and something I have never experienced.

Next, they take me to see my garden. Mom is on her knees planting. The ground is tilled. Some plants have been planted already. A few of them are already popping up through the soil. I see one beautiful white impatience flower with green leaves. I look off to the side and see rose bushes starting to bloom. Mom is so proud and I can feel her love. They also take me to my house. Now, there are six lights on, three on the left and three on the right. One light is on outside. The door has changed to gold.

From here I find myself in front of twelve beings behind a white marble table. Dad and Enoch stand behind me. The recorder and an angel in pink are off to the right side.

Again I feel I am being asked questions. I don't know what it is about but I can feel myself searching inside for the answer. It is as if I just dial up the answer.

Now I must leave with an angel. I go to a cleansing place. It is much like standing under a shower of silver energy beads. This wonderful energy falls all over you and yet you never get wet!

Another angel in pink shows up. They each take my arm as we move quickly. We are in a huge open area with tiers of seating in a circle. Many others are there. I again hear beautiful music. It is angelic and my whole-body tingles.

From there I am on a lake in my own sailboat. I can feel the sun and wind on my face as I'm sailing. It's a wonderful feeling.

I see Denny, an old college friend, and he tells me he's looking forward to me coming home.

Now I'm in a classroom with others. We are here to deprogram from the past. There is a blackboard in front of the room. It has numerical quotations on it. We learn how to apply them.

Then a gap... and I'm in a contest with other people. They are waiting for someone to come announce the winner. They haven't arrived yet. Someone asks if the queen is here. A man sticks his head through a curtain. He makes a motion to "cut the microphone" across his throat. He asks, "Who has the number 1 answer?" I raise my hand and go forward."

*****

After each of their meditations, Patty and Ron would discuss them. It helps a great deal to have someone to help process all this information. Often it is overwhelming!

Chapter 11

There was really no way for Patty and Ron to know exactly where all this was going. They could only keep doing what the universe was instructing and discover the result. They didn't even know whether there would be any other higher teachings. Soon that would all change. In the meantime, Patty tried to meditate every day.

So, February 1, 2011 started with a meditation. "A white winged horse comes for me. I get on and he shows me there are seven levels of darkness below the earth plane. It is darkest at the bottom then each becomes lighter as you move up. The levels above range in color from red to purple-the levels within them relate to the density.

We enter the purple level. I see many souls waiting for me. Some I know, others I don't. Aunt Mary greets me. I see Mom; my grandmother and grandfather are with her. They seem excited to see me.

Dad and Enoch are there. There are twelve White Brotherhood beings lined up behind them in rows of two. I am being taken to my house. They follow behind us. We are outside the house. I am being taken inside but only to some rooms downstairs.

It is beautiful inside. As you go in the front door, the floor is white marble with gold specks in it. I go into the first room on the left. For a second it looks empty. Then in a blink, I see built in bookcases filled with books. There is a fireplace with a fire going. The furniture looks so comfy. An afghan is on the couch. Above the fireplace is a beautiful painting.

Across the hall is another room. It is empty and to be filled later. In the hallway, I see a beautiful gold spiral staircase leading upstairs. I am not allowed upstairs yet. It's time to leave; more will come later.

Once again, I find myself in front of the twelve beings. Only this time I am wearing a gold robe. I'm wandering ... I'm being reminded that like everything, even our exit points are planned. Then Dad comes in, there is a gap, and I'm gone."

*****

Patty realizes that whenever someone dies and goes into spirit world there is a great deal of preparation that takes place. These higher-level teachings that are being given can show us all what we can all do here on a day to day basis. It's so easy to get caught up in our everyday lives that we miss what is really happening.

The next meditation came in on February 3, 2011. Once again it is food for thought. "I am in a canoe going down the river. I dock on the right. I look across and see many souls on the left. As I get to the end of the dock, there are gold steps going up. At the top is a white and gold door. Inside are rooms that all come in a circle. There are meetings going on in them. It's a place of very high-level energy.

I go into the third room on the left. I hear the word, "orientation". There are others in the room sitting in an L shaped table. We are being taught about the physics of energy. It is necessary to understand because it will help in the dynamics of utilizing energy in the spirit world.

When it's over, we file out of the room. Dad, Enoch and another being is with them. He is introduced as Father John. He was a priest on the earth plane and now devotes himself to transmitting universal truth. He will help be the go between with Ron and me when it's technical with the matrix numbers. He will help create the link when he's needed. He is very thrilled to work with us and says he has been waiting a long time for this opportunity. He was present when I was in the classroom where all the equations were on the blackboard.

Also, he tells me we feel unbalanced because of the recurring planetary issues. We should feel better in the next day or two. That's why our meditations are so important. Each meditation acts like a healing for us.

Who Am I ...... Really?

The connection that Ron and I have is so strong that our communication will come easily.

What Ron has agreed to do in this incarnation will reach many souls. He has no idea of his impact. When the time comes he will be ready."

*****

Patty and Ron would discuss this information while doing self-evaluation. One key to utilize is to stay in the present moment. Try staying in the present moment; it's not as easy as it sounds. In a matter of minutes or even seconds Patty would find herself either thinking about something that happened maybe yesterday or wondering about tomorrow. She constantly has to bring herself back to the "now" moment.

Here it is only the beginning of February 2011 and Patty can't help but wonder what will happen next. What she discovers only compounds the shock of what keeps happening.

On February 5, she and Ron were at the beach. For them, it is their playground. There is no total relaxation like the ocean. Couple that with meditation and the depth to which you relax and you have almost a pleasant coma state.

*****

"There is a spiral staircase leading up to the clouds. I go up the stairs and the clouds lift. I see a city and hear, "city of gold". Everything is covered in gold.

Dad is with me. We walk down the main street. He says, "This is where you'll live. You've earned it".

There are many cities on many levels. Each has its own energy level and pattern. It all fits into the matrix. The number of this level is 33.

Each city consists of its own matrix on a minor scale. Yet it all works together. Think of a crossword puzzle. You must get the words across as well as down to make it work.

This high level is what you have worked for as a soul. You had to clear the numbers to gain entry. You have no idea all the numbers you have cleared.

I ask where we're going next and he says, "There are more questions for you." Only this time I'm in the place where the white marble tables are located. I'm standing in the center. On each side is a table with twelve beings seated there. I hear the voice of the moderator.

(It is explained that each time questions are answered; a part of the soul energy returns to source. Again, they inform me that I have surpassed what I came in here to do. Now I am merely tying up loose ends. There will come a time period where I'll find it difficult to stay in the physical world. I will feel very scattered and lost, but that is all part of the process. There are many souls who will benefit from my experiences through transition. It will ease the confusion and bring peace to many.)

What Ron and Patty agreed to do together is to aid those in transition. So many fear the lights going out when they die. When the time is right, Ron will bring forth this information that will enlighten everyone.

I see Ron talking to a television host. She is holding up a book that we wrote together. I can hear her interviewing him. She asks, "What made the two of you write the book? How difficult was it for you knowing that Patty was leaving?"

From here comes Ron's book of numbers. She wants him to do a show teaching transition. The scene fades out.

I'm back in the Sacred Gardens. Father John appears. He is the link with numbers. For now all that is necessary is being done.

There is programming within Ron during dream state so that the code within him is activated at the correct time.

Each day brings new understanding and wisdom. The past is shed so new thought can come in. Number thirty-three is the master of spiritual consciousness, truth."

*****

Later that same day Patty meditated when they got home from the beach. "I see my mom in her nurses' uniform. She asks me to go with her. We go to a particular floor in the building. There are lots of rooms. It is the sixth floor. She goes into a room and I follow. She says, 'Put on a gown and climb into bed. They want to adjust your energy level." I am quite unbalanced right now. She just told me to relax. She tells me I will be there a while. I can feel my impatience kick in, then I zone out."

After these experiences, Patty is very surprised by all of it. Just seeing the City of Gold and then her energy being reprogrammed to help her, in itself is a great deal to process. Who could ever imagine that all this was real; yet it is all happening to Patty and Ron! They are both in a state of shock and it just keeps getting bigger. Both of them are merely your everyday normal people who each started a search and look what is happening as a result!

Chapter 12

The amazing factor in all this is that as these lessons come in, Patty realizes they are part of her life story. Most of us are taught to live life, get married, raise a family and finish out life. Patty had done all that and inside felt there was still so much more. That started her search for the meaning of life, how and where to find it. These lessons are her life story; yet it is everyone's story. They speak directly to her; yet they speak to everyone.

Patty's next meditation left her quite awestruck. That seems to happen more and more lately. It came on February 6, 2011. "First I get a flash of #66. I see Dad in his business suit and red tie. He says, "We have an appointment." I ask with whom and he says, "One very special soul".

We get on a gold escalator and start moving upward. It's a very tall escalator. There is a kind of white covering that hovers over top of us. It is almost like a blanket. When we get off the escalator, nothing looks solid. It's etheric.

A being appears. I know he has created form for my benefit. His energy is so elevated and so completely *love* that I kneel down before him in humility. He smiles and extends his hand to help me up. He asks me to walk with him. Dad stays behind.

Just being in this presence is too wonderful for words. I feel so honored. I know he is searching me inside. Any questions he has are being answered without me doing anything. I want to ask who he is but it doesn't matter. Then his thought to me says, "*I represent The Whole*".

We finish our walk and I'm back with Dad. I can only say that everything inside me is settled. There is a wholeness that exists within each of us. It is the quest of our search. Before now I had never experienced it. After being in the presence of this being, I found it.

I am whole; it was inside me all along. It is knowledge and feeling like none I have ever encountered. It is pure simplicity and a grandiosity all intertwined together.

We are back on the escalator. I realize I am not the same as when I went up. I feel very quiet. I look at Dad and he's smiling. I know he understands what I am experiencing. He takes me to an area where there is a beautiful waterfall. We sit on a bench and quietly listen to the sounds of the waterfall.

*****

The experience of this meditation was so profound, yet Patty wondered how long this feeling would last. One thing is for sure, no matter what, it had filled her inside with a peace never felt before.

The meditation the following day was very educational and it involved what is called the Hall of Records. It occurred on February 7, 2011. "I go through a tunnel. It starts out grey then turns blue, then turns purple. I'm in front of a large white building. I see Dad and Enoch. I ask, "What is this called?" I am told this is the Hall of Records. "Why are we here? I am told it is to give me more insight.

We go inside. This is a memory process. Just entering the energy within the building allows it to be released within the individual soul. This can aid them in understanding.

I am told many can search here to educate themselves on issues from their past lives. It helps them see where they could have made better choices and what growth areas where more work is needed. Those that have finished the cycle may offer to lend aid to those seeking help. For many, the answers are provided to their questions.

I see Mom; she's so proud of me and she wants to thank Ron for taking such good care of me. There are many there who are proud of both of us.

Father John appears. Look for meaning in numbers 33 and 66 and the connection. It goes back to ancient Hebrews."

*****

What is going on here? Where is this going? That's all Patty could think about. Plus, along with this, she is having more health issues. It's difficult to eat without feeling nauseated most all the time. The medication they gave her helps with cramping but she still feels lousy. It does seem that meditation really does help her feel somewhat better.

So, she continued and on February 12, 2011 once again she came out of it in shock at the events that occurred.

"I see Dad. He says there is a lot going on in and around me. We go to the picnic area and sit down. Next, we're walking beside the lake nearby. Dad spreads a blanket down on the grass and we sit down. I look up and feel myself letting go . . .

Now I'm on a silver train. Dad is with me yet when I get off, I'll be on my own. I look up and see a flashing sign. It says, "Final Destination". I get off the train and am not sure where to go. Ahead I see a sign that says, "Processing Center" so I go there. They take my passport papers and they stamp the date. It's in a circle and very clear.

"What does this mean?" I am told this is the date of your trial. You must appear in court. He says, "Bring your lawyer", and I see Dad. Then he says, "Until then you're free to go".

I walk away from there and see another sign that says, "New Recruits" and I go there. I walk into a room by the sign and it's a classroom with desks. There are a few others in there but the teacher hasn't arrived yet.

I ask if they know what this is about. One guy says it's about different opinions you have as far as what work you'd like to do while you're in the transition period from your life. The transition period is different for everyone. It depends on the maturity of the soul.

He looks at me and says, "Oh, you have a five-point gold star over your head. You're only here for three to five days.

Just then the teacher walks into the room. I feel very humble. He explains that new recruits are those in transition. It's a period of readjustment.

For some souls, illness has played a significant role and they need a long period of rejuvenation. Often that takes place in a hospital. For others, it is a brief period that takes place as a reorientation to the cleansing energy. There are three of us in here who mainly just need a recharge of energy. This is because we knew ahead of time about the passing and could prepare ourselves and those around us for the experience. It is also due to our soul level and advancement.

This made the transition quite easy. It removed a great deal of difficulty that would normally be present. It is as if we could preview everything and then we became the preview.

I ask what the next sequence of events is that takes place. I am told it all will come on a need to know basis. Then we are dismissed.

The teacher asks me to wait after class. Another being comes in and I am told there are more questions I must answer.

We sit down at a table and he begins asking questions and writes down my answer. I have answered three levels of seven questions and this is my fourth. We shake hands when he is finished and he leaves.

I find myself back on the picnic blanket. Dad asks, "How did it go?" "I think okay." He smiles and says, "If it hadn't gone well, you wouldn't be back here."

I see Mom coming toward us. She looks so young and beautiful. I hug her and it feels so good. They are so proud of Ron and I and what we have accomplished.

Mom said I had really learned and benefited from what she went through in her life. That was her role to play. But my choice was to learn from it or end up doing the same thing-not living.

I have questions but I'm not sure they can answer them. Dad says, "I can tell you this-after your final trial you will have a great deal more clarity and understanding. Until then, there's not much more I can say. It's just important to live out each day and enjoy it.

He says, "You will have the opportunity to see the kids again and say goodbye. The time you and Ron have left on the earth plane is very special. Cherish it. Sing, dance, and laugh, for it will carry you far.

When the time comes for you to leave; your connection to him will actually be stronger than what you feel on earth. It will be a soul to soul connection link. This happens only as a result of the individual and collective work you both have done. You will be very pleased with the results.

You actually are entering the door to heaven and have the ability to bring parts of it back to share with the world. That's all for now princess. We love you very much."

*****

Patty can't help but think how strange things were becoming between the teachings, her meditations and how she felt physically. Talk about overload! So much was going on inside her head and all she could do is try to sort it all out.

Chapter 13

The realization of what really goes on between these two intertwined worlds is mindboggling. The shame of it all is so many people are misdirected through all the various teachings, either through church, television or many other avenues. The reality is that *everyone* can experience all of it themselves. Once that happens, they will have truth! But for now, Patty and Ron just have to keep plugging away learning and meditating. Hopefully their result will be enough to help others who are searching as well.

For Patty, the next meditation on February 13 was equally profound. "I'm in a garden area. There is a huge waterfall surrounded by large rocks. I'm leaning against a rock. I hear someone coming. Its Dad and Enoch, with the recorder behind them. They have something to tell me. I have asked for clarity and understanding about what is going on inside me. I feel changes much like an upheaval but don't understand it.

Enoch says, "What you feel are changes occurring on a physical, mental and spiritual level. You have reached an agreement on a soul level as to the point of your departure. It remains within you for now. You have plenty of time. Use what you feel and trust it. For all purposes, you have completed what you set out to do and more."

Now I'm in a church and wearing a gold robe and gold crown. I go down the aisle in this church. I am seated on a throne. There are twelve elders who stand behind me. There is a white lamb in front of me, and an eagle is to my right. I am told, "This is your sacrifice."

There are four stages. You're in stage two. I ask what I must do and am told to be patient for healing must take place. I ask, "What else can you tell me?" I am told, "The time will come when you will have the opportunity to say goodbye to those you love. Many will reap the benefits of your path of transition. It is important to document your feelings as you experience them. This will leave your mark in the world and help relieve many fears. The masses fear death because of the misinformation that is being distributed. What you experience will help to change that. This will be your testimony."

Now I am in a canoe paddling down a river but allowing the current to take me where I need to go. From there I am with Dad and he takes me to a counter inside a building. I ask, "What is this?" He says, "This is where you come to sign in." I see my name put on a list to be picked up. There is a date by my name but I can't read it.

Then I'm back at Dad's house. There is a contract on his desk. It has a gold seal on it and reads, "Expiration date of June 15, 2011". I ask about it. Enoch says, "This is when energy around you is removed and dissolved. It deals with the past and projects that you agreed to undertake. This is removing residual energy and anything left incomplete. By removing the energy your transition will be easier".

Now three angels appear, two in pink, one in purple. They tell me they will be with me from here on out. They help prepare me for what is to come. It is explained that I received education also in dream state. They help also to prepare me for my upcoming trial.

Next, I am in a room with the angels and the recorder. He is writing in my book. There are not many pages left. They tell me I will feel moments of many varieties of emotions. They will be with me to help when needed. I see number 42, 77 and 144.

For now, it's just important to live in the moment and enjoy all I can. I am so grateful for their presence. My journey is complete.

I ask about Ron and am told Ron is known in the spirit world as a teacher for those to watch and learn from him. There are souls who must reincarnate. Because of Ron's level of awareness, they are sent to him. A few come close to let him know they are here. There are many others watching in the background as well."

*****

Something Patty realized is that in the meditation where she and her dad are on a picnic blanket; she can feel herself letting go. This is the same as zoning out. Only in this instance she has full recall to bring it all back. Other times she zones out and can't remember anything! She realizes she is not allowed to bring it back. Sometimes it also depends on the depth of the meditation.

*****

Her next meditation added a whole new twist. It occurred on February 14, 2011. "I'm waiting at a bus stop. A yellow bus comes and I get on. Dad is talking to the driver. I ask where we're going. He says, "There's more for you to see."

It stops at a large building and we go inside to a classroom. There are students in here learning how to levitate objects. Also, they learn how to create the objects they are levitating. Like everything here, it is through thought that creation takes place. I notice some people do it easier than others. They say all it takes is practice.

It is also being explained that when a soul first arrives they must orient themselves to their surroundings. In the beginning, there is always a guide or angel with them. This enables the adjustment period to flow much easier.

Depending on the maturity of the soul, that determines how long they are needed to help. A truly involved soul will have no need of help because they have done this thousands and thousands of times. Some also just want someone to be near them. It also depends on what the soul has accomplished in the lifetime.

If they are detached it is smoother. If they are attached to any person or place, then it takes longer to reorient themselves. Help is always there when needed. Also, for a person who has been misinformed on the death experience, it means a great deal more help is needed. Those who are free of attachments have the smoothest period.

I am told my journey will flow easily because of the work I have done.

Again, we're moving. Dad says, "We're going to the Gold City." I notice how the energy vibration is greatly elevated. At this point I went so deep I am unable to bring back anything."

*****

Patty had been received channeled higher teachings which she has mentioned. You will find them all in published together in a new book, so that their meaning will be on a understood on a deeper level.

The next higher teaching really helps both Patty and Ron to have more understanding about life. How often do you have a plan for your life and then you quickly discover that what has happened is nothing whatsoever that was any part of your plan? In other words, your life didn't work out anything like what you thought it would! What Patty and Ron were finding out is that they would think in small detail while the plan of the universe is far greater than they could imagine!

*****

Patty and Ron decided to spend the day at the beach. Here's what happened during her beach meditation. "Ron and I are standing at the alter in a church. He's wearing a grey silk suit, red tie and a white rose boutonniere. I am wearing a white wedding dress and carrying a bouquet of white roses.

Our hands meet in the center between us and are placed over top of each other. On top of our hands is a white dove. It flies off and a huge shaft of white light comes down. I rise up into it. I turn around to look at the church and I'm not there; only Ron is standing at the altar."

*****

Patty was left speechless after this meditation. She had just seen herself move into the light to spirit world. When she turned around to look, her physical body was no longer there. All she can think is, "Okay, there is no denying what just happened!"

*****

Now, just the following day, the 16th, Patty again meditated at the beach. It seemed that the more she saw and experienced, the more real it all became. It is almost like reading a story, her life story. The more pieces she had, the easier it is beginning to fit into the puzzle.

"I see Dad's briefcase with GFS in gold letters on it. I'm going through a tunnel, blue then purple. There is a pure gold light at the end.

I'm standing in front of my house in spirit world. I look around and I'm alone. I see Dad coming from one direction and two angels dressed in pink coming from the other direction. I'm facing the front of the house. The two outside lights are on, six lights downstairs and two lights upstairs in the front of the house. The upstairs lights are on the left and right side of the house.

I ask if I can go inside and am told not just yet. It's not time but will be soon. My time here is limited and I see #41 and 82.

I ask when I am leaving and hear "around 6-9 months". Ron and I are to celebrate every day we have left.

We start moving and I ask where we're going. I'm told it is a special rejuvenation place for mature souls who just need a tune-up and removal of residual energy left from their crossing.

It is outdoors and formed with energy fields. When you step into the area you literally feel the level and balance of the energy. This is where I will come instead of a hospital setting. My awareness and acceptance has earned this point of orientation. There are other souls present here.

Dad tells me I have a meeting at 3 p.m. with the elders. We go there now (no time and space in spirit world) and at 3 p.m. a part of my soul will leave. They ask me questions in order to discover in-depth analysis. I am confident in providing the answers correctly. We finish and I leave.

Now we head for Level 6. We move quickly. I have an angel on each side holding my arm. Dad is behind us. We cross over the energy boundary of Level 5 to Level 6 and I immediately see little sparkle lights all around me. It is as if I was standing under a shower. It feels so wonderful!

As we move along we pass others. I can see their aura colors and recognize the purity of it all. Here it is explained that creating a home or anything else is merely a choice.

Some souls want a place to go; others are satisfied just being present in the energy. Sometimes a soul may choose to create a home and then after a period decide it's not needed, so it is dissolved. It is all about choice.

The level of comfort I feel is magnanimous! It is nearly time to leave. The angels each take my arm and we begin moving. They tell me we're going down to Level 3. First, it is to readjust to the energy of that level and from here I will travel back to my physical body. Once my energy has adjusted, I am placed in a chute which sends me back into the tunnel.

I feel so grateful for all I have experienced. I get ready to come back and I notice the recorder is writing in my book. I look at him and he says he will see me later.

I keep going and feel myself returning to my body. A white dove appears on my left shoulder and then another appears on my right shoulder. They both fly off at the same time."

*****

Ron and Patty continued to have surprises, both in dreams and meditations. On the seventeenth of February 2011 Patty had a very short piece of a dream that truly was an experience. "To the right of my belly button is a mass. I can hold it between my hands and feel the size of it. I ask Ron to feel it."

Patty really doesn't know what to make of all this. Is this a premonition? What else could it be? For now, she pretty much blew this off.

They decided to spend the day at the beach relaxing and here is the meditation she experienced.

"Dad says my suitcases are all empty. I see it go from black to white. "Okay princess, today we celebrate". I said, "Celebrate what?" He says, "Celebrate your completion of all levels necessary". You completed the last of it in dream state last night. You need only now to go through the rest of the process to reach your final coronation".

"It's much like solving a puzzle. You have it all finished except for three pieces. You know exactly where the pieces go but it's just not time yet for the whole puzzle to be revealed. It's all about the timing and alignment with the universe. Plus, you have things you need to do on the physical level there, so you will have that time. When everything is in sync, your final destination will come in. Until then just relax."

I ask what the three puzzle pieces are and am told one is the final trial, two is the final review and three is the final meeting and questions on my level of attainment. They are very pleased with all I have accomplished.

"Both you and Ron need the time to fortify yourselves both individually and collectively. You both have a great deal of work to do together, just not in the way you anticipated. There are still big plans for you both.

I see several former presidents and one says, "Congratulations are in order. The universe rejoices in your honor."

Again, I am in a room with 18 beings. I stand in the center with them forming an upside-down U shape. They begin to ask me questions. As I answer I feel the energy of my soul respond. For now, I just am to realize all that has transpired. My journey here is almost over. They anxiously await my arrival. As I continue to write and as I put it together even more will be revealed.

I may look back in wonderment for what has transpired but not in regret. I am told, "You have learned wisely."

Ron needs to know that his place for teaching will come in only when it can be resurrected and not before. Those who would destroy it will be gone.

Mom comes in to let me know there is nothing I can do for any family members unless they ask for help.

Dad says, "We'll cut this short, you need to rehydrate. We all love you."

*****

Now, in the midst of all this, something else is also happening. Ron's mom has decided she wants to sell her house and move to Florida. The house has been on the market for about nine months. There were a great deal of showings, but no offers. The first realtor they had was not the least bit aggressive in trying to sell the house. When the contract ran out, Ron and Patty found a realtor with a great deal of sales experiences and many closed deals.

Of course, she had ideas to improve the house so it would sell. Ron's mom needed to move some furniture out, paint, update, etc. She really couldn't get the help from family there that was needed. So, it was looking like Ron and Patty would be going north to help get things moving there. It seemed like their plates were really filling up!

On February 18, 2011, Patty and Ron again went to their favorite playground at the beach. The meditation Patty experienced was quite earth shattering and brought a new level of understanding.

"First I see #55. A blue and white magic carpet picks me up and we go out into the universe. I see a star straight ahead and we move toward it. Next, I see a city of lights that look like crystals. We land in a field of wild flowers.

Then I see an outdoor cafe. Mom and Dad are sitting at a table all dressed up. Dad is wearing a blue silk suit with a red tie. Mom is wearing a pale blue suit and a navy wide brimmed hat. They are so happy to see me. I ask, "What's going on today?" Dad says, "Just relax and be patient."

They want to talk to me about my accomplishments. First and foremost, I had to learn to stand on my own two feet! In doing that I helped my children to do the same. Then I had to find my belief system and philosophy rather than just going along with the masses.

Doing these two things allowed me to clear up some past lives. I also had to feel my emotions instead of repressing them. I had to learn to recognize my anger and know that it was okay to let it come out. These characteristics have served me well.

A great deal was realized through all this. Above all, I have truly learned the meaning of unconditional love both in giving and receiving. Recognizing the difference between those who need help and those who want help was a turning point, along with accepting people just as they are, without judgment.

For now, we finish here. I ask, "Where do we go now?" Dad says, "To see what you've procured."

Next, we're out in front of my house. The downstairs lights are on, eight of them. I am allowed to go inside the front two rooms downstairs. I walk into the room on the left. It is beautiful. There is a fire place with a fire burning in it. The energy vibration is a deep purple.

Now I see a party taking place there. Many people are chatting within the groups. It is as if I am observing but not a part of it. I don't think they know I'm here.

Dad is beside me. I ask if we can see the other room and he says, "Yes". We walk in and I see the ceilings must be over ten feet tall. There are book cases built from the floor to the ceiling. It is filled with books. I feel excited and Dad smiles at me. He says, "Within these books you will find only truth and boy will you be surprised!" He wants to show me something so we must leave.

We go out and there is a portal. He tells me to look in the portal and see what's going on. I look down and see a graveside burial taking place. A minister is present and other people are crying and sobbing. He asks, "What do you think of it?" I say, "I think it's silly". "That's right", he says, "Look at the anguish and pain in the widow and her children. This is what you will help change. You must address this in your writing. It is about celebrating life and celebrating death. There is no need for mourning." It is merely the energy of the earth plane that feeds death as a denial of truth. You will see more later. Come back then and we will finish."

*****

So much is happening it feels as if Patty's head is spinning. There is so much information she and Ron need to process and try to understand. Patty can't help but reflect on the meditation. Seeing the funeral really hit a nerve. The biggest funeral Patty remembers is her dad's. Any funeral she's ever been to, everyone just tries to keep from falling apart!

The truth is that if everyone had the information Patty is being given, then death would truly be a celebration! All she can think is, "Oh, if only I can help to open people's eyes!"

Chapter 14

In the meantime, Patty feels the importance to keep meditating and learning. Each day seems like an epiphany that keeps on coming!

Her beach meditation on February 19, 2011 brings even more understanding. "I go through a tunnel with purple mist. On the other end is a rail car. Dad is in it and beckons me to hop on. I ask, "Where are we going?" He says, "A lot has been planned."

I see three angels off to my side and they come close. We begin moving and I am told we're going back to Level 6. I can feel the energy vibration rise as we go through the levels. I find myself sitting in a garden type setting. It seems tropical. There are flowers all around. Dad is beside me and the angels are behind me. I feel we are waiting for someone special.

A being appears as white light. I am most humble in this presence. Words cannot express the love vibration that emanates here. He can see into my thoughts, my mind. I can feel questions are being asked yet no words are spoken. The answers merely present themselves. I have never experienced anything like this. I think, "May I ask who you are?" I hear, "**I am the right hand of the ALL That Is.**" Again, I am so very humbled.

As we finish, this white light energy merges with mine and it is incredible! Just like that, he is gone. I look at Dad and I see by his smile that he knows exactly what I'm feeling. I can hear harp music. I turn to look around and see six angels playing harps.

The three angels touch me and I know we must leave this beautiful place. This experience is extraordinary to put it mildly.

We begin to move quickly and are back in the picnic area. Dad and I are sitting at a table. 'What was that", I ask? "That was your first incarnation into spirit world. There are two more of these to come".

I feel as if something within me has changed. We sit quietly for a few minutes as I try to process and let things settle.

Dad asks if I'm ready to go again. We take off and in a blink, we are at what I'll call a construction area. He tells me I will see how it works. There are people here and one is in charge.

Dad tells me he is known as "Ben, the builder. His mind is open so tap into it and tell me what you see."

"I see in his mind a blueprint of what he is constructing. It comes in flashes of scenes to the finished product. As I view it, it is manifesting."

This was Ben's occupation in his last incarnation. I ask Dad, "How did I do?" "Great!" he says and laughed. "Often new souls have difficulty getting to see all the details but you have it right down to the plumbing!" I can tell he is pleased.

He explains that the lower levels carry an energy of structure, which is solid to touch. It is similar to what most souls are used to in early maturity. With each level gained, the energy becomes more fluid. All can see and experience this when they are ready.

Now he says we must leave. He wants me to see the research area so we take off again. Soon we are in what looks like a scientific laboratory area. He explains this is where souls work with those on earth to find necessary cures for illness that has been created.

This work cannot interfere on a karmic level. The reason for the research is to combat or balance what the darkness creates. An example would be a major epidemic occurs and the energy of those affected builds on panic. In helping to find a resolution, it will help balance the energy. Those meant to make their transition from an illness for reasons of karma; that will still happen.

Creating resolutions merely helps keep a level of universal balance. There are more explanations and understanding to come later.

Self-imposed cures are the best cures of all but the earth plane as a whole is nowhere near ready to accept illness merely as a dis-ease. They prefer to give power to the medicine gods as they say, for healing.

It is much like the church goers giving their power to religious doctrine, ministers, etc., when religion has absolutely nothing to do with life. It is all merely a form of brainwashing.

Only when everyone begins to search inside themselves can real harmony and balance occur. They're just not ready.

Dad says, "I know this is a great deal to take in but you're doing really well. The more prepared here you are and the more prepared on the earth plane, the better it will be."

I am told to tell Ron to just relax and not judge what he's receiving. Just take it in and he will understand later. He gets too frustrated when he can't understand what is received. When that happens, he is to just take it in; it all has purpose. Put the frustration in a box and put a lid on it. Please!

"Well, princess, out time is about up for now. We are so proud of you both. Love from us all!" Then I see a gold chalice and #66."

*****

What's interesting now is that Patty's meditations seemed to be longer and filled with a great deal more insight and understanding as well as resulting in still more questions. She figured she could only wait and see what would happen.

On February 21, 2011, she and Ron were at the beach. It was so easy to meditate there and the wind, sun and sounds of the waves only added to the depth of relaxation.

"I see a huge white ship and a gangway leading up to it. Dad is at the top of the gangway and motions me to come so we can board. The name on the side of the ship is the S. S. Hope. We board and immediately go through a purple mist.

I wonder where we're going. Dad says, "There is a portal in the ocean to the other side at 59 degrees". It is like going through a tunnel. We come out the other side and it's clear and sunny. I see a port ahead.

We go there and I see merchants selling their goods at an open market. Dad explains there are masters among the common people who have chosen to come in to help others. He says to look into their eyes and you will know them by their soul.

Immediately, we are levitating. The three angels are with me. I ask where we're going. They say, "To gain more knowledge".

Up ahead I see an energetic barrier. They take my arms to move me through and Dad is behind us. I see a portal and they tell me to look into it. As I look down I see the inside of our condo. Ron is helping me into bed. I lean on him to help me walk. I am weak. I see where I've been to the hospital. I'm seeing things in reverse order.

Next, I'm out in front of the hospital sitting in a wheelchair. Ron went to get the car. I had been on a floor and had IV's in me. I was being released from the hospital after surgery. I see a male doctor with dark wavy hair come into the room. Ron is sitting in a chair by my bed. The bed is by the window.

I can tell by the doctor's eyes-he says there is nothing more we can do. "How long do I have?" He says, "Six weeks at most". I tell him I just want to go home. He says, "Okay, we'll give you something for the pain." I knew all this was going to happen and now it's surfacing. A nurse comes in to check on me to see if I am okay. I tell her I'm fine.

"He's writing up your discharge papers and then we'll get you dressed".

I see Mom and Dad step into the room. Ron knows they are there too. They just offer their support.

Now I'm back in bed. I realize I want this time alone with Ron. I am so grateful he is with me through this journey. Now the scene fades.

I see myself as violet energy. The angels take me back to the room where I met with the council. This time I am merely purple energy. As I look at them, there are 18. I just see gold and white auras. They tell me I am ready for Step 2.

All this is predestined. Again, there are more questions. I feel answers surfacing within me. When they are finished, I feel my energy from the questions dissipate. I am finished here for now. I am so relieved.

I see Dad waiting with a big grin on his face. I see how proud he is of me. He tells me there is a great deal for me to process and for Ron too. I know not to ask for a time frame because it would not be revealed.

Dad tells me Aunt Daisy has invited me to tea. In a blink, I'm at her house. She hugs me and we go out into her garden. There are beautiful flowers everywhere and iris in every color! There is a table set with beautiful china tea cups. We sit down and she tells me how glad she was that Ron and I came together. She says he has no idea how special he is and that my love for him allowed more of him to open up, so more could be brought through to him. "You might say you helped put him on the fast track." It is only a result of the work we've done on ourselves.

I am grateful to have had this time with her and to spend it in the energy of these beautiful flowers.

I see Dad waiting out front. I thank her and leave. Dad says, "It's time to leave", and we take off. I ask where we're going and he says, "Just one more special place".

It is a place for children and babies. He explains these are souls who changed their minds in utero or those who died as infants. Here they grow and prosper. There are angels here and fairies as well as nature beings. I also see nurses where needed. It is a very magical place and I am honored to see it.

Dad says I must go back now. He takes my hand and the angels lift from behind. I see them all helping me gently back into my body. I thank them all and send them love. I see number 44 and number 144. Dad says, "Just take time to process what you've learned today"."

*****

The next day, the 22nd, Ron said he had a dream he was single because I was gone.

Later that day Ron and Patty went to the beach. The meditation Patty had there was about showing her how things work while being an observer. It involved the number 77 as well.

"I'm waiting at a bus stop and a white taxi pulls up. The door opens and I see Dad inside. I get in and he says, "We'll use this portal today to enter spirit world". Next, I see the taxi surrounded by a thick purple mist. We end up outside a building that looks like an air terminal.

We get out and I ask where we're going. Dad says, "There are some things you need to see". We enter a small room that is like an observation area. We look through the glass in front of us.

I see many souls arriving. They each have someone with them, either a guide, angel or loved one. I am amazed at the huge number or souls.

Dad says, "This is merely a fraction of them". He asks me to look at them and tell him what I see. What I notice most of all is that just by looking at them I can tell whether their energy is depleted and by how much.

I can see whether it was a long or short illness, merely old age or suicide. I can see how much rejuvenating they will need. Dad says, "You're doing really well. These souls will be processed and either sent to a hospital or resting place for rejuvenation. Some also go to orientation and on to the level their soul has attained.

Dad explains there is always someone with a returning soul. Since they still carry the attributes they left earth with, some are open to new knowledge and wisdom while others remain either completely or partially closed off. The choice is theirs but someone is always close by to help them.

I ask where we're going next and before he can answer we are moving. I see myself in front of an alter wearing a gold and purple robe. They seat me on my throne and place a crown with jewels on my head. Eighteen beings surround me. An eagle is to my right. A man's face is to my left and a lion is behind me. A white lamb is in front of me still alive. I am humbled.

There is a huge shaft of white light that flows down and engulfs us. What an experience! All that I see and experience is part of the process. The more I learn, the more comfortable I become.

Today I am reminded that what I experience will be a catalyst for many souls on their own search.

Everything in the work Ron and I do, our books, teachings, everything will be encoded. Merely through hearing, teaching or simply by reading; the vibrations of the code will be activated. In this way, an opening can occur on a global scale. Merely being in the presence holding one of the books will alter one's vibration.

It begins what is almost a magical process of healing through the vibration of words. There will of course be many skeptics that will challenge the authenticity of it all. Those closed to it will remain closed. Those who experience the change will be the witness of it all. They far outnumber the skeptics. Ron will enjoy their skepticism and prove truth where it is needed.

Celebrate today for it is a turning point in both your lives. Well, your coffer seems full for today. Take time to digest and process what has transpired. We all love you. Dad"

Chapter 15

Ron and Patty wondered if any other teachings would come in the rest of the month. In the meantime, they were still trying to figure out how to help his mom with the sale of her house. It was as if all the energy toward selling her house stopped moving. What was weird is that there were so many people who had looked at the house and yet not one offer was even presented.

It was a beautiful condo with tons of room, located on a golf course and well decorated to her tastes. They just couldn't figure out why it wasn't selling.

The only thing that made sense was that no one there wanted her to move. Everyone thought she should stay put! They believed she'd never be able to sell her house. So, all this energy was being put out to keep her there. Patty and Ron were the only ones who supported her decision to sell the house. It was very sad.

However, the meditations continued and seemed to go in new directions. On February 23, 2011, the silver train came once again.

"I see a silver train coming. It stops and I get on. I see Dad and one of the former presidents with him. "I brought a friend along. He wanted to meet you", he says. I am honored.

We sit down and he says, "There are so many who talk of you and Ron. I just wanted to meet you in person while I had the chance. The two of you help people to open up whenever they have contact with you. Your work is very impressive and will help many souls". I thank him. The train pulls into a station and he gets off. He tips his hat as goodbye.

Who Am I ...... Really?

I ask where we're going now. "We'd just like you to spend time here and get used to it". He asks if there are places I'd like to go.

"The stables, so I can see my horse."

The train stops and we get off and start moving. In a blink, we are there. It feels so good. "What are you naming him, Dad asks?

"Dancing Star".

He shows me a huge riding ring with jumps set up. "Here you can ride to your heart's content".

When I'm ready to leave the three angels appear. We begin to move again. I find myself in front of my house. The downstairs lights are on as well as the front lights upstairs. But the back of the house upstairs is dark.

I see an old medium friend, from the days I took classes. He's smiling big and glad to see me. He says our isolation is necessary to remove barriers we don't need any longer. The healing work is allowing the barriers to come down. He is proud of us both.

The angels lift me and we begin moving. Dad is behind me. "We're going where you can have an energy healing session", he says. The next thing I know I'm lying on a table and a huge scanner with light moves up and down my body. It produces a mild tingling sensation. Dad says, "It helps balance your energy because of the work you're doing on yourself." Now I see a violet light in the scanner. It flows over me. I'm being told we still have time.

The repositioning of my energy over there is what causes me to feel scattered. They balance me to make it flow more easily.

I slip on a step, not sure where I'm going.

Dad takes me to a picnic table by a lake. We sit down. He tells me they will keep repositioning my energy. For now, I just relax and let go."

*****

Now more than ever, Patty and Ron were beginning to realize just how much the meditation is giving to them. It is total self-healing every day! They are giving themselves a gift just by taking this time to meditate.

Still they wondered just how this information would be presented to others. Would anyone even be interested? Yet the depth of what they receive seems so difficult to grasp.

After discussing each meditation, Patty and Ron are left to ponder their own lives and events as well as what they share. It can be overwhelming, and yet they feel the insight being given within all the knowledge. There is a wonderment of what would come next. Patty's meditation on February 24, 2011 provided some insight.

"I start down a staircase and in a moment, I'm sitting in Dad's office. He is behind the desk across from me. Mom is sitting beside me.

"Why am I here", I ask?

"We want you to know some things. First of all, you need to understand the importance of all the information you're receiving. You've read the book, *The Blue Island*, and that was written many years ago.

What you and Ron are doing is providing a present-day version. Not only that but you are providing step by step details of the death process while you're going through it! It hasn't been done before. Although there are similarities between the two, it is the modern-day wording that will jump out at people; you are the average soul making your transition.

Since you can see and experience a great deal before your actual death; when people read your testimony, it will cause a questioning inside which helps them open to possibilities.

Whether they believe it or not; they will still question. The purpose is just that once they begin to question, openings will occur.

Ron will have to write part of it as you're going through it at the beginning of the death process. Then once you're settled here, you can channel the rest to him.

Everyone here is very excited about this project and all the possibilities that will result from it.

Ron is going to be very busy both in his own work and book as well as the work you created together. He will speak in many places about both your experiences.

We want you both to know how important it is. We're finished here for now and we'd like to show you some more.

First, there are some doctors and healers we'd like you to see." In a blink, I'm outside a room with two doctors. They have me stand against a white wall. They merely look inside me. They explain they are looking at my astral body but can still see into the physical body.

They see black and green in my upper intestine; smelly stuff is draining where it's not supposed to be. I can smell a very strong foul odor.

I see number 42 on my body on the lower abdomen and 62 on my upper abdomen. They explain that they are allowing things to progress while keeping the discomfort under control. They will tell Ron when it's time to see the doctor. We will both be prepared for all this.

Patty, you will notice little things that happen and it's important just to make Ron aware of what's happening. The closeness you both feel with each other will be far greater than either of you could imagine. It's just important to enjoy each day. That's all the writing for now, just relax and let go."

*****

This meditation helped them to begin to realize the importance of this project. Hearing their words along with the energy of the meditation gave the fuel to keep going and trusting in the universe for results.

Patty's meditation the next day, February 25, provided her with the possibility of what job she would be doing once she was over in spirit world. Could this actually be something she might be doing?

"I am the pilot on an airplane. There is a co-pilot with me. It's time to land. I land the plane and get off. I go through the terminal and security.

Next, I'm in an airline club room. There are other pilots here and we are in a training session. It is explained that we will be flying other passengers to different realms of existence. I am the newest pilot in the room. Other pilots have already made some trips. I am told I will not start this until I'm ready. They are merely preparing me.

The training ends and we are dismissed. We leave and I find myself in front of my house. Dad and two angels are waiting for me. "How did it go, "he asks?

"Okay, there was a lot to process."

"It's okay, you have plenty of time for it." "Would you like to go into your house?"

"Yes", I reply and we enter through the front door. It is gold. I stand in the foyer. There is a beautiful staircase. It has a blue and gold rope across it. I can't go upstairs yet. The house is fluid. I have permission to go to the back of the house.

I go toward the back and into a gorgeous kitchen with skylights and a large center island with a sink in it. It's beautiful. "What do you think?"

"It's wonderful, but is it necessary?"

"You earned all this but you can change it whenever you wish".

We go out the back door. There is a round patio made of bricks and there are roses, gardenias and daisies everywhere. Dad tells me they planted some of my favorites and I can do the rest.

It's time to leave. I see the man with the white beard. He asks me to go with him. Dad is behind me.

I am being asked questions again. The energy of this being is so high and I bow in reverence. I feel that what he asks is regarding my departure. I know I can't bring it back.

The answers flow easily to his questions. In each moment, I am confident. Now, I'm vibrating and slipping away..."

*****

Here it is the month of February and usually it seems like a short month. Yet for Patty and Ron, with all the information in meditations, the month seems to go on forever.

On February 26, 2011, they were again at the beach. They found that just spending a few hours there gave them the relaxation they needed. Also, it relieved any stress that would tend to build up.

"A white winged horse appears. I get on and we take off. We go through a dark tunnel and come out into a massive white and gold light. There is only light around and in us. There are other people here. I see Dad and he comes over to me.

He explains that while I am in this particular energy, it is helping to give me balance from the scattered feelings that exist. He takes my hand and we start moving. I want to ask questions but decide to wait and see what comes.

The three angels appear and the next thing I know is that I'm sitting on my throne. I wonder why I'm here and they say it's part of the preparation.

I am handed a gold key and told it's the key to my house here. While I don't feel the house itself is important, what is important is what I've accomplished to reach this level.

Next, I am back in dad's office. Mom is there with several other relatives. It is so good to see them all.

Dad says I will feel the presence of those close to me all the time. Someone will always be there to help. Ron takes care of me in here and they take care of me over there.

He says for several months I will be fine and then I will begin to see more subtle changes. It won't be all at once but a little at a time. The time I have here is very special.

It is explained that I am on a timetable so to speak. The events are already written. The schedule can change in time as in moved up or delayed, but the events will occur. For now, the timetable is what is orchestrated.

It is important to listen to my body. There will be doctors around me as well. It will be an easy transition for me. "When", I ask? I am not told anything.

Dad says, "Right now it would do more harm than good to know". He wants me to meet some others.

Next thing I know we're in a huge banquet room full of people. Dad is introducing me. I see several former presidents, musicians and many others I don't know.

It is explained that these are all people who in some way are part of the work we do. Some may only play a small part while others have a much larger part. It is quite overwhelming.

"You really have no idea how important it all is and how it ties together. The work you do will affect the masses and be carried lifetime after lifetime."

Ron and I will be spending more time in dream state learning and preparing. Dad says they will only give us what we can handle.

We leave and I am overcome with a lot of emotions; all these people are counting on us. It is our gift to the world but the reality is that it is a gift to us as well.

"That's enough for today", Dad says.

I see the white winged horse and climb on his back. "Goodbye", Dad says. The angels rise and surround us as we travel back.

*****

One thing is for sure, after that meditation, Patty and Ron begin to realize even more the importance of what they are doing. They sure didn't understand all the reasons, but it definitely got their attention.

Only two days left in February but without a doubt, the end of the month was momentous.

Patty's meditation on February 27, 2011 occurred at the beach.

"I see a silver escalator going up. Mom and Dad are waiting at the top. They are all dressed up. I ask where we're going.

"We need to get some things out of the way", they said.

We move quickly. We're in a room with three other beings. It is hearing about me. Dad is talking to them about what is planned for the future. He has everything mapped out. He is submitting it for final approval. I see the date of April 11 and ask, "What's that?"

"Your transition is made up of four steps, he says. Some are physical, some emotional-mental and some spiritual. The 11th is the first step. He is asking that this plan be approved and they place a gold seal on it.

"The second step is the trial on May 26. During the trial, the mental and emotional will be brought into the spiritual". I will transcend to that when the trial is completed. It is a merging through realization.

"Step three will occur on August 9th". By this time, I will notice significant changes in the physical body. As this occurs the astral body will become more acute. All this will come easily.

I see some documents on the table and ask what they are. I am told they are the first three steps.

"May I read them?" "Yes".

The first explains all that I have completed. I see a list of numbers. 42 is at the first and the last is 144. It states I am aware of what is going on and am informed. I sign it.

The second is about the writing and what I've agreed to do and be part of. Dad says, "It's your project". I sign it and see June 8th.

Number three will be signed later. There will be more preparation and teaching first. I sign number two and we are finished here.

The three angels appear and mom says she must go. I hug her and say goodbye. She tells me everything will be okay.

I feel relieved to be through with all that. We take off and the angels are on each side of me. They each hold an arm and we move up through the layers. Dad says he will wait for me.

We travel through the layers and I am met again by a highly evolved being. He just says, "I am Light, names do not matter". I feel very relieved. He simply says, "You have done well, my child and we are ready to receive you".

"What more must I do?"

"You will be lead every step of the way. We ask that you merely live each moment. The lessons will continue for you to spread throughout all. You are blessed."

He walks me to the boundary edge and the angels await me. We begin to travel back down through the layers and Dad is waiting.

He takes me back to the picnic area and we just sit at a table. He is beaming at the events which took place. He explains that when a soul is open it is so much easier to prepare them. When they are not open there is much more confusion and much more teaching and preparation that must take place.

"That's enough for today", and in a blink, we're back at the escalator. He hugs me goodbye and says, "I love you princess" . . . and I go back down the escalator.

*****

Well, after that meditation there was no way Patty and Ron would deny what was happening. Although they had no idea how important this project was, they sure do now! Patty realized that we agree to do things long before we ever come in here as incarnates.

Only one more day in February and she wondered what else could happen in her meditation. She is about to find out.

*****

"I hear beautiful orchestra music. I can see a white and gold staircase leading up and I walk up the steps. Dad is there at the top and takes my arm. He says, "We are going to try a moving exercise. I'll help you if you get stuck. Picture yourself outside you house here."

Just like that we move and are outside the house. I can tell by the look on his face that I did well.

"Now, use your key to go inside". The same number of lights are on. There is a huge beautiful bouquet of flowers on a table in the foyer. We go back into the kitchen and another bouquet is there too. "It's a welcome gift", he says.

"Now, picture yourself out back in the garden". Again, in a blink we are there.

"Okay, think of the picnic area where we sit and talk". Quickly we begin to move there.

Dad says that I did an excellent job. He explains that going through the layers takes more practice and we will try that another time. I see a Master and the recorder.

"He would like some time", Dad says.

We go sit down. "There are only a few loose ends to tie up. Your trial in May will finalize the loose ends. By then the teaching and most of the preparation will be completed. He explains that over the coming months I will go back and forth in sleep from sleeping very sound and deep to sleeping a few hours, being awake, then a few hours of sleep, etc."

The entire time they will be adjusting me for departure. I see the recorder and ask what he wants. "I am merely present", he says. I see him writing and there are fewer pages left.

I am told they will help coordinate the book and I am grateful. "It is already written", he says. I ask what else I need to do and am told I'm already doing it.

He tells me to make a list of who I want to say goodbye. It is much more for them than for me, for it will be a shock to many.

"We are finished for now", he says.

I am being given a little at a time so I can process and accept it. I thank him. Dad takes me back down the staircase and we say goodbye.

Chapter 16

Patty and Ron had shared all that happens in their meditations. Patty is amazed at the means of travel in spirit world. She was pleased that she could follow her dad's instructions. Also, she was very glad he is pleased as well.

The beginning of March once again found them on the beach. They loved to search for sea shells and were always on the lookout for dolphins. Several times the dolphins had come close to them. One day they even could have reached out to touch them. That's how close the dolphins were to them. It was an unforgettable experience!

They continued meditating at the beach. Here is her meditation for March 1, 2011.

"I'm sitting on a bench waiting for a bus. A tour bus pulls up and the door opens. Dad and Mom are sitting behind the driver. I go up the steps and turn to see my relatives and Ron's relatives are on the bus too.

I sit down across from Mom and Dad. There is a guide on the bus with a microphone. He's explaining there are levels which all relate to one's belief system. If they are closed, they go to a level which appears most like the earth they left. Only when they seek to open and educate can they begin to move toward a different level.

Several lower levels relate to more solid structure. The higher levels relate also to the advancement of the soul. The more advance, the higher the level.

The bus stops and we get off. I ask Dad where we're going. "To a new class", he says. The next thing I know we're outside a classroom. He says he'll be waiting there when I've finished.

I go into the classroom and it is quite crowded. I take a seat and a teacher walks into the room. He will be talking about the matrix. At the front of the room is a blackboard which has the matrix on it and its constantly moving. You can see the numbers changing.

He explains that according to universal law, there must be a balance where negative events occur; there is also a balance of positive events. Each one affects the whole and it must be kept in balance. Everything must have balance. The weather must be in balance-floods and cold versus calm and dry. Clouds and sunshine, windy and calm must balance. It all provides balance.

Each life has its own ups and downs to be in balance. The cycle of having everything and losing everything; it provides balance.

Everything is in constant motion, which is how the universe works. This understanding is a key for each soul. It also helps to go beyond seeing ones' self as a victim. When one can attain that realization then many doors can open. It is all about self-realization.

Our class is finished for now. I go out into the hall and Dad is waiting for me. He takes me to my house and we go inside.

He asks if I'd like to furnish the two front rooms. "Yes", I say.

"This is another exercise in creation. He tells me to picture what I'd like to put in the room in vivid detail. Now, hold it in your thoughts and focus exactly how you'd like it, what color, size, texture, etc. Now imagine where you'd place it in the room".

I do it and he says, "Now, place it there and then let it go". Just like that I see a couch and table I had pictured. I continue to do this until it's completed.

It does take considerable energy to focus and do this. Dad explains that the more practice I have, the easier it becomes. "We'll do the other room another time".

Next, I find we are in a kind of hospital exam room. He explains it's merely to recharge what is depleted from the exercise. He goes on to clarify that a great deal is going on with Ron and me. Many changes are occurring as part of the whole process. We both need to be sure to meditate every day. It really is important.

"We're just going to take some time here", Dad says. "Today will be mild because there is a great deal of adjusting taking place. Giving too much will result in overload. You are at a saturation point".

So, that's it for now. He walks me to a white gate and opens it. I go through the gate and he must stay on the other side."

*****

The vast information that is being received is quite overwhelming for both of them. Often when they discuss it, they end up speechless. Really, it just needs to sit with them so they can try to process everything.

The next day they went back to the beach wondering what else would happen in meditation. The date was March 2, 2011.

"I see an escalator going up and I take it. Dad waits for me and I can see he's in a hurry.

"What's up?" I ask.

"We going to be late", he says.

"Late for what?"

"You'll see".

We get on a silver train and it's as if we go into a thick cloud of fog.

Next, we're moving and then inside what looks like a huge coliseum. It is filled with people.

"What is this?" I ask.

"First there will be a kind of teaching. This is very special and for a select group of souls. You must be ready to receive it or you can't be here." He grins and I am honored.

"You won't be able to take it back with you". I am disappointed but I understand. We sit quietly and I absorb it all.

There are four beings down in front. They each play a role. I can see the auras of what is being delivered. I can see the colors as they emanate from them, deep, deep purple, gold and white. The energy is amazing! It is like watching a stage show of lights. I can feel the energy being absorbed into me. When it's finished, the stage revolves and on the other side comes a grand orchestra.

They begin to play the most extraordinary music like nothing I have ever heard before. It encompasses all that I am.

I am enjoying this so much!

Dad explains that there was a great deal going on yesterday and so they decided to make today lighter. I am grateful.

When it is finished we leave. He asks if I'd like to see the House of Music and I say yes.

We move and go into another huge building. It has an open foyer at least three stories high. In the center is the most beautiful grand piano I have ever seen.

Dad tells me that any instrument you can think of is here. Anyone can learn to play any instrument they wish. There are always teachers here. I am thrilled. "Often, he says, souls have always wanted to play an instrument but never did. So now they have the opportunity. You can come here whenever you wish."

We leave and he tells me we have a meeting to go over some more questions. Again, I find myself in front of eighteen beings. Everything is by thought and they search for my answers. These questions decide how the preparation process is going and to see how ready I am to receive more.

They tell me I am right where I should be in this regard. They are working with both of us at night also. The more prepared we are, the easier it becomes. We are doing exactly what we are supposed to do. I express my gratitude and humility.

We leave here and Dad helps to move me. Next, we are in a small coffee shop. Mom is waiting at a table. It seems they like meeting in cafes and coffee shops! I can tell how pleased they are. Dad says, "After the questions, we just wanted to bring you here so you could relax in this energy".

"That is enough for now. Go back and enjoy your love and the rest of your day".

I hug them both goodbye and find myself going back down a tunnel and into my body."

This was quite a meditation and Patty felt it seemed to be happening a lot lately. They spent the rest of the day just enjoying the beach and doing a great deal of talking.

*****

There was so much that needed to be done on Ron's mom's house and no one else seemed to offer to help. So, he called his mom and told her we would come up to paint, strip wallpaper and just update things. "We'll leave first thing in the morning", he said.

His mom was so grateful and so relieved. Little did they know what was really going on up north!

They went home, packed up the trailblazer and headed north early the next day. It is a seventeen-hour drive so they split it into two days. Even with that they were pretty wiped out when they got there.

They had no idea how long they would even be there. His mom was just glad they came to help. There was furniture that needed to be removed from her sewing room, wallpaper taken down and neutral paint in several rooms to update the house. It was quite a bit of work. All this was happening with house showings on very little notice.

Patty and Ron also came to learn that most of the neighbors didn't want her to leave. They thought she would never sell the house at all. Some even thought she should wait before she even put it on the market. They felt she was making a huge mistake. They honestly didn't believe that she wanted to move to Florida at all! It didn't matter that she told them otherwise. It was crazy! This was the energy they were up against.

All this came as quite a shock to Patty and Ron. They thought everyone would be thrilled for her to head for a climate that provided much better weather and a much healthier lifestyle. Boy were they wrong!

Plus, there were numerous comments that some neighbors had the idea not only that she didn't want to sell at all, but was being forced to do so!! It didn't matter that she told them she couldn't wait to sell her house and move to Florida!

Now they began to understand why the energy to sell the house stopped flowing. There were too many people surrounding her that wanted to keep her there!

After several weeks, things were looking good. Plus, in the process they helped her get rid of anything she didn't want to bring to Florida. Merely three weeks later, she received an offer and the house was sold.

Now began the task of packing everything up for the trip south. They had people load up the moving truck and Ron drove the truck while Patty and his mom followed behind in her car.

During this time, with all these distractions, neither of them could meditate and therefore no teachings were received. It took a toll on them just be being so out of balance. Also, it was a very stressful situation.

They could only hope things would improve once they came back to Florida.

*****

The month of March was quite strange to both Patty and Ron. They were glad to be able to help his mom. Yet they were completely out of their routine. They missed meditating a great deal. This was a time when they were really embedded in the day to day life. In itself, that was strange. But it also provided some great learning experiences about people, life in general and it showed them what a different life they lived.

With everything Patty and Ron were involved in with the sale of the house and packing; they knew it would be some time before they could get back to any type of regular routine, let alone meditate every day. But it was all necessary.

Chapter 17

During the rest of March and most of April, Patty and Ron had been packing for the trip south. Once the house closed the end of April, they began the trip south.

For Ron's mom, it was a fresh start in a totally and completely new setting and lifestyle. For Patty and Ron, it was much more than that!

Patty had found some time ago that in a meditation she discovered a past life she had with Ron's mom. In that life Patty had been homeless and starving. She was an orphan who was living on the streets. Ron's mom took Patty into her home and heart and raised her as if she was her own daughter. Now it seems Patty would have the chance to pay her back.

His mom moved in with they and they put most of her belongings in storage. They wanted her to be comfortable for as long as she wanted to live with them.

So, for the next few months she became a very large part of their day to day lives. They truly enjoyed having her live with them. Eventually she wanted a place of her own where she could meet people her own age and start living life! So, after a month or so, they began helping her look for her own place. It really didn't take long.

Fortunately, they were very lucky and found a condo in a wonderful retirement community just over a mile from their condo. It was perfect. So, her new life was about to begin. They did some painting and once again loaded a rental truck with all the things she brought down for her new home.

For Patty and Ron, it was now time for them to once again get back to their disciplines of dreams, meditation and channeling. Hopefully more lessons would be received.

It really took longer than they thought for them to get back into their normal groove. Just trying to remember and journal dreams took some time. It was nearly the middle of May before things were back in a normal routine.

On the fourteenth of May, Patty had a very shocking dream.

"Ron and I stopped for gas. I asked if I could use my credit card. A woman said she'd see if it would go through. I went to pick up 6 bottles of 7UP but there were only two of them there. Then I went to pee. A woman was waiting for my credit card and I said, "I'm sorry, I really had to pee".

This dream points out Patty's need for meditation. The woman is a guide. Credit card is something I'll pay for later. Urine is releasing emotions. There was a real need to release. Patty went to pick up 6 bottles but there were only 2; meaning 4 were empty, finished. This is a short dream that spoke a great deal.

The next day, another dream even pointed out what was going on around Patty.

"Ron and I are walking along a river bank. The water is muddy. I look across and see 1 turtle, then 2. Then I see 1 deer and then I counted more deer up to 20. This dream tells Patty that she is unable to see clearly due to emotional upheaval (muddy water). Deer are gentle aspects of self. Number 20 is the world of spirit and matter, associated with resurrection and reincarnation. Turtle is the need to slow down. Also, 20 deer is a merging and reorganizing in both worlds.

It finally began to look as if more teachings would be brought in to Patty. She is just beginning to come to some terms as to just how enormous this project was going to be.

Only six days later another teaching came in the early morning hours. For Patty, it is a huge responsibility. There is no going back to sleep once this happens.

*****

Patty would really be relieved when this trial was over. As if to play some catch up for the time they were up north, the rest of May continued to bring more telling dreams. This next dream about a week later, the 24th, dealt with Patty leaving.

"Ron and I are standing in church with a large crowd. We are singing a hymn. I can't see clearly. The man in front of me takes a step to the right so I now have a clear view."

The church is seeking guidance. Singing is harmony in a situation or relationship. Singing a hymn signifies the dreamer's death. A step to the right is opening up.

*****

Even after all these years of dreams, it still amazes Patty how things are presented and orchestrated. It felt good to finally get back to regular dreams and meditations. The following day, Patty had an early morning experience that revealed a great deal.

"Early this morning a circle of six beings came for me. Dad was with them but outside the circle. Enoch was one of the six. I am levitated up and we move over into spirit world. As we move, a gold energy flows into my crown chakra. I am taken to my house and find myself upstairs in an incredibly luxurious bed. It has white marble pillars on each corner.

Mom comes in her nurses' uniform. I receive a healing I also see a large circular bath and hot tub. When we leave, Ron is waiting outside the front door. He is not allowed inside. Also, Dad gives me a golden horseshoe."

*****

Two days later, May 27, Patty received a channeling which provided her with a sense of accomplishment and a great deal of relief. Her trial was finally over!!

"Congratulations! It has been completed. More will be shared with you in the weeks to come. We celebrate all that you have accomplished here. You have come very far in your journey. There are other necessary steps that will occur in due time.

The council is pleased with your responses and you will see the significance of your endeavors.

The next week or so you will find many shifting energies around you. Try to stay in a state of fun and relaxation and it shall ease the process. More will be explained as it is experienced.

Your father wishes a moment. "Congratulations princess! We are all so very proud of you. Ron needs to relax about all this; he gets too keyed up. Many unsettled details were completed last night.

Patty, you can help things along just by being patient when you speak. We expect the offer on the new condo to be put in early next week. (This is the new condo Ron's mom was buying). Use tomorrow to resolve any unanswered questions. She just needs to get her toes in the water and she'll be off.

Utilize what you need to help make her more comfortable with it all. Remember, for her this is new and scary. Each time something comes forward that she hadn't thought of, then another resistance falls away. Arming yourself Patty, with all the information you can acquire will help a great deal. Rest assured all is well. Blessings are yours, Dad."

*****

May 29, 2011 brought a short dream with a great deal within it.

"Triplets are being born-not mine. I go to the hospital to see them. I'm going down a long hallway. Five doctors dressed in blue come around the corner and go to them. They are born. You can hear them through the intercom."

This dream is about the spiritual birth of the trinity. It also involves a long transition.

So far, the month of May had been full of events that astounded both Patty and Ron. Yet it still wasn't over.

Chapter 18

Patty was being taken on a trip. It came after a channeled teaching on May 29, 2011. She wondered where she would go and what would happen.

"A ring of beings surrounds me and we rise through the layers of the universe. There is a night sky with a million stars. I can see my star. I am wrapped in a blue and purple mist.

We're in front of a large building. This is a class for orientation. It is for those entering a new level of development. Everything is deep purple. In the center of the room is a gold shaft of light. I am to stand under this shaft.

I can feel this energy reaching every cell of my being. As I step out of the shaft, it is as if I am glowing. I see several people I know.

Now we leave this building. Dad and a master teacher are with me. I go before 24 elders and am asked my final questions.

I am in a church sitting on a gold throne. There is a gold crown of jewels on my head. A lamb is in front of me. It has been slain and blood drips from it. I am wearing a white and gold garment with deep blue on the front. Eagle, man, ox and now slain calf.

The church is full of people. I stand and a shaft of light pours down on me. It is the purest energy I have ever experienced. My journey has ended.

I am in bed in my house in spirit world. Mom is there in her nurses' uniform with two star beings. Dad sits in a chair by the bed. He has papers he's going over with me and asks me to sign them. I ask to read them with recall.

"This is your final declaration of life. June 16, June 25". I ask how much time I have. Dad says up to six months from then. You may choose at a later date. I sign the paper.

Many people start to come into the room. I see many relatives and friends. They're all dressed up. My aunt sits on my bed and gives me a hug. They all want me to visit with them.

It is time to leave for now. A ring of gold surrounds me and I am lifted. We come down through the layers."

*****

Patty and Ron couldn't help but wonder after all this, what would happen in the month of June. It seemed difficult to find enough time to do the writing and meditating. Patty had questions about the teachings that were missing or out of sequence. Still, she knew she was just the channel. She just needed to keep clear and let everything flow.

So far the first week of June had been quite busy with teachings. Yet Patty was finding out that there are not as many dreams she remembers. Still there is just so much information it is mindboggling.

*****

After another channeling, Patty was taken on another trip. It was June 7, 2011. She couldn't wait to see what would happen. It was all so exciting yet overwhelming!

"I am lifted up and we move through the layers. I find myself walking in a forest. It is dark because of all the foliage. In the center of the forest is a shaft of white light. I walk to it. As I get to the center and stand in it, the light grows. Everything around gets bright and the shaft of light leads straight up. I am moving up.

We cross over into spirit world. Dad and a master are with me. They take me into a large building. It is the hall of records.

We go into a room. Outside there are windows with counters. Behind the windows are people to help you. We by-pass that to enter a room. There is a large table with a chair on each side. I sit on one and the keeper is in the other.

There are five gold books on the table. These deal with this particular lifetime. He takes the first book and turns to the last page. He stamps it with a gold seal and passes it to me to sign. The date is May 6, 1991. I sign it and pass it back to him. He closes it and puts it off to the side.

He goes to book #2 and stamps the last page. The date is November 23, 1996. I sign it at the bottom and it is placed on top of book #1.

He goes to book #3 and stamps it. The date is June 1, 2004. I sign it.

He goes on to book #4. He opens it and stamps it. The date is April 21, 2007. He places it on top of the others. These dates are when they were completed.

On the cover of book #5 is a gold buffalo. He allows me to read it. It all flashes before me in a millisecond. He places a stamp in it but there is no date yet. It is not time for me to sign it. He takes #5 and puts it on the shelf. The rest of the books he carries out of the room to be stored.

As I get up to leave the room, a gold mist forms around me and again I find myself back in the forest and walking out of it.

*****

All Patty could think was WOW! What more could you say?

Today is one of those days when Patty's head is spinning. "I feel as if my head could explode from all this knowledge. I only hope I do what I'm supposed to do in the best possible way. Yet all I can do is trust in the universe and whatever it has planned for me."

June sure is going to be an interesting month. Patty wonders what will happen next. Some days she thinks, "I really believe without a doubt that I am leaving". Then two days later is could be, "Am I crazy?"

Almost as if to answer her thoughts, the universe provided more confirmation that is hard to deny. Patty's meditation on June 9, 2011, left her speechless.

"Hello princess, it's good to be with you. Let's take off so you're elevated, okay?

I am in a blue and gold bubble being lifted up through the layers. I land on a train platform. The train is waiting for me. Dad is already on board. I get on and the train starts moving.

He has some more things to go over with me. We stop at a huge terminal and go down a long hallway.

Now we're in a conference room. Dad shows me more documents. I'm trying to read them and it looks like a type of plane ticket. On the top it says," entrance visa doc". There are three copies. I see a date of June 17. He tears off one copy and hands it to me. I realize when I get the third copy, that's it.

For now, we are to just take care of Ron's mom. Make sure you keep the lines of communication open with her. Once she is settled in, she will have a new lease on life. Her apprehension comes from not knowing how to do things. She doesn't have to do anything; the new life will come to her.

Patty, your job is nearly finished there. Still some loose ends to tie up. Seeing your kids is very important. They will have grieving to do but they will deal with it.

Well, I think that's enough on this right now. We all love you. It'll all be okay, Princess, I promise. Love, Dad".

*****

This meditation left Patty a bit bewildered. What's interesting is that while she's in the meditation, it feels almost too real to put into words. Then she comes back into everyday life and can't help but feel some doubt.

So many feelings and emotions go into it and despite the doubt, how and why would all this information come through it if weren't truth?

As Patty continued to question, it seems the universe was providing the answers.

The next day, June 11, she had the following dream related to her leaving.

"I'm going to an outdoor concert with two girls. There is a man who lets you in for good seats. It costs $10.00 to get in. The first girl says she'll take care of it.

Ron is leaving with another male and sees me. He's glad to see me and we start kissing really strong. Then he leaves and we go in and sit down for the concert. There are a lot of people there."

The dream deals with harmony in a situation with the inner self. I need to sit down and contemplate a situation. The $10.00 is karmic closure, completion, and rebirth. Kissing is love, affection harmony. Everybody is aspects of self. I'm finally in the center of self. Three walking in is the trinity. Ron goes in one direction and I go another. Its spiritual harmony.

*****

The month of June continued to be busy mostly with meditations coming in along with some dreams and channeling. It seemed as if they were making up for lost time. The ten teachings Patty was supposed to receive in March were delayed when they helped Ron's mom move. Now it seems they were coming in June every few days.

Once again Patty had a very brief dream that was quite enlightening. Still she was unsure of its exact meaning. It occurred on June 15, 2011.

"I know I am on Level 7. When I came back in, I looked down and said, "Oh, this is what I needed to wear to be on Level 7."

For the next week or so, Patty received a teaching every few days. Talk about overwhelming! The time that was lost is definitely being recovered.

She realized that all these experiences she was having would give knowledge and hopefully a comfort or sense of peace for anyone who might be interested.

*****

The summer months for Ron and Patty are wonderful! Oh, sure many people complain about the heat and humidity, but they love it! It really isn't any warmer in Florida than it is up north. Plus, you always have a breeze coming from the Gulf of Mexico. Pure and simple, for them it is paradise!

In the meantime, the condo Ron's mom bought is due to close the middle of June. So, they have been shopping for furniture and trying to remember exactly what she had put into storage.

The good thing is that Ron and Patty had moved so many times, they felt like professionals.

Chapter 19

The month seemed to be very busy between moving, shopping and getting Ron's mom ready to move into the condo. They were all over there every day. Ron would haul the boxes while Patty and his mom did the unpacking. Going from a four-bedroom condo up north to a one bedroom condo here provided some challenges. Basically, it was, "Where in the heck do you put everything?" But it was fun trying to put it all together!

June was over and Patty wondered what would happen in July. It seemed trying to find time to meditate could be a challenge.

July is one of the hottest months in Florida. People would talk about being inside in the air conditioning. Then when they went outside into the humidity, their glasses would steam up. Patty and Ron didn't care, they loved all the weather, the hotter the better.

So, the beginning of the month started out with Patty beginning to journal more dreams. Of course, they still pointed to her leaving. The first dream occurred on July 9, 2011.

"I'm on a trip and outside. There are chairs in a row. We're up high. I sit down and say I need to get new sunglasses. There are vendors in a circle. One girl says there is a man who sells them but its a couple hundred dollars. I say I'm thinking more like twenty dollars. I get up and go look but don't see any sunglasses.

She wants to take my picture and I say," Then I'll take yours". We go where I'm standing on the beach with the ocean behind me. The sun glistens off the water. It is the most beautiful picture."

This dream deals with the view being in spirit world. Number twenty is between the two worlds. Vendors are undergoing changes in waking life. Circle is perfection, completeness, immortality. The sunglasses protect my perception so I can see clearly. Picture is how you see things at this time. Ocean is life force, sun is Christ light within, and the beach is the bridge between the physical and material worlds. It is my view from spirit world."

*****

As if a scene viewing from the other world wasn't enough; this next dream is one which shows Patty over in the other world. It occurred on July 11, 2011.

"I've been gone and am back. I'm in a house. The house is familiar yet nothing inside is familiar. I'm sitting on a couch. I look at the floor and there is a floral rug. I ask, "Did we buy this? Ron said, "Yes".

I'm upstairs and there is a support beam and when I touch it, it breaks off. I realize it's only a foam beam and put it back.

People are in and out of the house. I feel so strange the whole time. The way the government runs things is so different; almost dictatorship.

Finally, I ask someone, "What year is it?" "2054". I get really upset with Ron because he didn't tell me. He let me think I was only gone a short time.

From there I had to go see a movie. I file in a theater with others, all males. They file in and sit down. You sat in every other seat. I end up sitting on an aisle seat. The man next to me doesn't like me sitting there. I get up to find another seat. I go toward the back and sit down.

There are two men sitting together with a coat over them and I know they're masturbating. I get up and go stand in the back and lean against the wall."

This dream points out that Patty isn't recognizing that she's leaving. The movie is looking at life. There is a need for release of stress (masturbating). The wall crumbling is whatever she had in the past crumbling. People out of the house is sprit world, there is no free will there. Patty should be going forward instead of going to the back.

The fact that she leans against the wall are barriers she puts up, blocks, and obstacles.

There are permanent cycles, one for the natural in here and one for over there.

*****

As if things weren't strange enough, on July 12, Patty had another component to add to it all. It dealt with the pattern of the blue lights.

"Just as I was waking up, the patterns of the blue lights changed. They have always been in a certain pattern that is squarer in shape and overlapping as they flow around me.

Today, they arrived much smaller in size, almost circular in shape yet each one individual. Still they flowed in a string, one right after the other, all over and around me. It was a noticeable difference. What could this possibly mean?"

Another dream occurred on July 18, 2011.

"I'm at a television host's summer home with others. I had been at a previous one. We're outside in an open area. She called out to me and said, "Chris Backmann's book had shit on it. I hope you washed your hands after you touched it."

I thought a minute and realized it was from the other time I was here. I said, "I washed my hands after I handled it."

She said, "Come walk with me". I did and we started walking. She said, 'We could go on the boardwalk".

I wanted to ask her how long she comes to her summer home but knew it was none of my business so I said, "I just love it here!"

The next day, July 29, 2011 Patty received the following communication from her dad.

"Hi princess, I'm glad I caught you. Things are progressing well over here. Now the two of you have another busy day. Try to be sure you have plenty of energy through food and even a few moments of recharging your energy. Use the tools you know to do this and I guarantee you won't be exhausted when you reach home.

Again, there is a great deal going on from here in your dream state. Yes, Patty, we'd like you to begin Monday on the book for an hour or so. As you simply read it, you will begin to formulate a plan of putting things together. Just take your time. Try to ease through your day without rushing. It helps keep your energy balanced. When you take off in a hurry, your energy is depleted, especially Ron's. That's it for now. We love you. Enjoy your day. Dad"

*****

The very next day, the 30th, Ron told Patty, "last night I heard my mom say to a man, "My oldest son Ron is going to handle my affairs when I'm gone." Ron said, "You mean Patty and me" and he turned around and I wasn't there.

Patty realized you just never know the ways that information comes through from the universe.

July had been quite a month of learning, insight and information. The last day of July provided still another dream which showed Patty moving over into spirit world.

"Ron and I are going to dinner at a special restaurant. We go through a waiting area. I see a lot of people I know from fifth grade. I don't remember all their names. I go say hello to an old friend from high school.

To get to the eating area you climb this very high ladder. It's the highest ladder I've ever climbed. As I reach the top I see the blue sky. There are 4 men, one on each side of the ladder. They say they'll help me bet over the top. I ask how many steps are left to go down on the other side. They say, "Only 4". I said, "Oh, that's not bad." They tell me exactly where to put my hands and how to shift my weight to the other side. I get my right leg over and finally pull my left leg over and go down the four steps. I realize Ron isn't there and I am alone. I look up and see the blue sky and below is the ocean."

In this dream, the waiting area is the soul level. The ladder is rising above the human conditions. Eating dinner is independence, acceptance of others. The restaurant is seeking nourishment, outside support. Fifth grade deals with being rid of the earth self. The four men on the ladder are four angels who help me. They give instructions as to how to do it. There are four steps needed.

The blue sky represents the world of spirit; the ocean and beach are the bridge between the two worlds. This dream shows me going up the ladder, moving over into spirit world."

*****

As if that weren't enough, Patty had another dream the same night. It was quite brief yet it revealed an enormous amount.

"Ron and I have all these tickets and we have to assign them numbers." Tickets are new experiences.

When I told Ron about the dream and the tickets, he got a flash of number 144. This dream dealt with having all my tickets for my transition and assigning all the numbers.

The month of July ended and the more Patty learned, the more truth seemed to come out of it. Denial had no choice but to take a back seat.

Chapter 20

August began with meditations that indicated what Patty would be going through here on earth. It began August 2, 2011.

"Something was shown on the left side of my abdomen, some kind of battle. Then someone reached down and lifted something over my head. Then I am gone and a Holy being was there instead.

I see November and I'm in bed. That's about all I can do. October will be very busy and then the hospital and home. Ninety days from crossing is when it begins.

Part of what will make me sick to my stomach is the transfer of energy from this plane to the next. They will make it as easy as possible.

Some dietary changes are coming in September. Bland food will be what I want. I see a gold crown inside my aura over my head. They want us to relax."

Even though Patty is given specific months, she has come to learn that we really don't know what it means. First, in order for something to manifest in here, it must happen first in spirit world. After a great deal of frustration, she has learned to take in whatever dates are provided and then see what changes in here on a physical level. Many times, the changes are extremely subtle.

What she is finding is that from an energy pattern, she has slowed down. Some days she doesn't have the energy to do much of anything. So, just taking a wait and see attitude gave her the means to let go and avoid the frustration.

*****

The next day, August 5th, Patty had another dream about her leaving.

"I'm in a dream and see and old high school friend and a few others. She's there to tell people she's dying and leaving the earth plane. She has a long receipt and I look at it and say, "Well, you're not the only one leaving. I'm leaving too". "What illness do you have?" Then I wake up.

This dream was quite clear and straight to the point. Our dreams are orchestrated just like everything else.

*****

Her next meditation brought a quick review of her life and the time she spent with her mom.

"I see a gold staircase before me. Dad and three judges are waiting at the top. I go up the stairs and feel nervous. But Dad is smiling at me and he winks.

We go into a room and I sit before them. There is a screen behind them. I see my life flash on it and in a blink, it is over. They congratulate me and shake my hand.

Then I'm in a garden and an old college friend in spirit, is with me. Mom and my grandmother are sitting on a bench waiting for me. I hug them both and feel their love.

"The next six to eight weeks will be a bit rocky but we'll try to make it as smooth as possible. Once both your and Ron's acceptance kicks in, you'll find it easier. You're not there yet, but well on your way.

The way you feel physically is your key of truth. Enjoy all you can taste while you can because the time is coming where it will be more difficult to eat very much. Once you hear and find out where things stand, you will feel more of a sense of peace. Trust me on this.

There are so many who await your arrival and so many others who will learn from your experience. The two of you are presenting a great gift to the world. We are so proud of you. Rest when you can, you both need it. Love, Mom"

*****

The rest of August continued to be filled with meditations, dreams and teachings. On August 16, 2011, Patty had another shocking meditation.

"Dad is waiting for me. I go down an escalator then up twenty steps to a higher level. When I reach the top, he has his briefcase with him. I am escorted through a group of people. They are all clapping for me.

I am wearing a white gown with crystals all over it and a gold crown on my head.

After we go through the people, three angels appear behind us. I am escorted to a throne. I sit down and the three angels bow before me.

I see the date of August 22 and "Final Declaration" with a gold seal. "Declaration of what", I ask? Then I see, "Declaration of Life".

Next, I am taken to my house and when we get there the door is already open. I go inside and am told all is being prepared.

I'm in the bedroom and see clothes in the closet. They are not like anything I've seen. It is as if they are gowns but consist of assorted colors of energy.

Then a very high level being comes in with the following words: "Good day and welcome back. We have been waiting for your return. The loose ends have been completed. You have done well in your preparation. You have realized a great deal and we are happy with your accomplishments.

From here on out you will continue to see and feel changes occur. You are both ready and prepared for what is to come.

Take time to enjoy the fruits of your labor. Your connection will only solidify in the time to come. You have both reached a new level of awareness and understanding. Do not be afraid of it.

Patty, just listen to your body. We are here to aid you so call on us when needed. Cherish all you have. We cherish all you are."
"Wholeness"

*****

On August 20, 2011 Patty had another dream pointing to spirit world.

"I have a transparent glass Christmas coffee mug. I ask someone where hers is and she says, "Mrs. S. put it in the cupboard". I open the cupboard and look inside. Hers is in a white box. I want to use mine and take it out of the box. It's transparent glass with Christmas trees engraved on it. I'm just holding it."

The mug is nurturance and alternatively represents transcendence to a higher realm of consciousness. The Christmas tree is new beginnings, passage of time, spiritual development. Tree symbolizes growth, what you accomplished.

To open a cupboard signifies revealing a hidden truth. Mrs. S. was my neighbor growing up. I went to visit her in July and she passed into spirit world on November 28th.

My glass coffee mug going to her glass coffee mug is the connection to the other side. White is truth, new beginning; in Eastern cultures, it symbolizes death and mourning. Opening the box is self-discovery.

*****

Things really keep getting stranger and stranger. Patty listens to her body and is finding difficulty eating much. She can only eat small amounts before she has to stop. There is a great deal happening and still the dreams and meditations keep on providing insight.

On August 22, 2011 Patty had an especially powerful meditation.

"I go down many stairs. At the bottom is a gold tile floor. I'm standing in the center. Then I'm lifted onto a gold escalator going up. I go up four levels. Dad and Enoch are waiting. They take me to a room where a priest is waiting, Father John. He's working on the link between Ron and me so Ron can hear my thoughts.

Next, I'm lying in bed in my house in Spirit World. As I lay there I can feel pain in the stomach of my physical body.

A large winged serpent appears. I am not afraid of it. It's green in color. I climb on its back and it turns to gold.

After that I'm in front of 24 beings. They are seated at a white marble table. I am standing in front of them. There are beautiful grapes, bread and wine laid out in front of me. It looks like a feast. I take some of each and as I do a gold energy flows through me. I see number 144.

From there I am taken to Level 7 where I meet with a very high level being. The energy is so pure. "Are you ready for what is to come?" I answer, "Yes". I bow and feel very humble in this presence. He asks if I have any questions.

"Have things been moved up?"

"Does it matter?" There is my answer.

I am now in a garden and handed one red rose and one white gardenia, my two favorite flowers. The smell is intoxicating. It is like an amazing perfume.

I must leave here and am taken to a pool for cleansing. It energizes my soul.

Dad waits to take me back. As he leaves he hands me a red rose and I can feel his love."

*****

Patty is completely overwhelmed by this meditation. It seems as if each experience is more powerful than the last one. Still, it is difficult to process it all let alone comprehend its totality.

Even more insight was provided in Patty's next dream on August 25, 2011.

"I'm staying on the 2nd floor of a hotel before I go back for my last few months of college. An alarm clock goes off and I shut off the alarm. I take my suitcase and go downstairs to eat.

A man comes and said he wasn't sure I'd hear the alarm. I said, "I made sure I heard it. I only have a couple months of college left and I'm all finished." He tells me there are two places to eat. One is "Angels on 4". I decide to go to Angels on 4.

This dream deals with Patty's transition. There are only a couple of months left of learning. The 2nd floor is foundation, hotel is transition. College is how we learn in here. The clock is important moment in time. Alarm is fear there is not enough time to accomplish goals. The clock is stopped, end of time, death.

The man coming to tell me where to eat is a guide. There are only a couple of months left before I'm finished what I came in here to learn.

*****

Then the next day, the 26th, just as Patty was waking up, Ron said, "Last night you came to me and showed me a calendar. I pointed to the date, October 26th". Obviously, this means something but we don't know exactly what.

Merely two days later, Patty had another short dream.

"I have 4 baseball tickets". That was all she could remember but it says a great deal. Baseball symbolizes a team and individual sport. It can also deal with returning home to God. The ticket is "legal permission to enter". Number 4 deals with the earth plane. The dream is another indication of Patty leaving.

*****

That took care of the month of August. Despite sometimes feeling as though her head was constantly spinning, Patty couldn't help but wonder how things would progress in the weeks and months to come.

When was she leaving? How much would she know ahead of time? Each day delivered a great deal of information. However, who really knew what was coming next?

Chapter 21

The month of September in Florida is still quite warm and breezy. For Patty and Ron, it was a quieter time. There was much less traffic; most of the northern snowbirds had returned home. Going to the beach often meant having it all to themselves.

Beach days seemed to happen less and less due to their schedule, but that was okay too. As long as they were together, that was all that mattered.

For most people being together, twenty-four hours a day often meant conflict. For Patty and Ron, it was just the opposite. Being separated meant conflict. They loved each other so much and every hour of every day was precious.

For Patty, the meditations and dreams continued to point toward her leaving. Yet it was about this time when Patty woke up one morning and something felt very different.

"Something has changed", she told Ron. "I feel as though I'm not leaving this year like I thought. I think it has been delayed for some reason".

Now, Patty had nothing whatsoever to base this on, it was just how she felt when she woke up that day.

*****

Patty's meditation on September 1, 2011 let her know that some of what she's receiving she doesn't want to hear.

"I go up a white marble staircase with gold pillars. I'm in a room with a recorder. I can see very few pages left in my book of life.

Then I'm in a room where I'm meditating and lying on a bed. Ron comes in and pulls a large gold shade down behind the bed and one on the right side. I see he's on the phone.

He takes off my headphones and I wonder what in the world he is doing. He hands me the phone and says, "You have a phone call". I take the phone and say hello. I hear several people all talking in the background but I can't hear them clearly. I say, "I can't hear you". They try a better connection but it's not good.

I get off the phone and get up. I hear a lawnmower. I put the big shade up and look out the side window shade to see where the lawnmower is but I can't find it."

*****

The shade offers protection and the fact that it is gold is Divine consciousness. Patty is being brought into divine wisdom. It is the acceleration of the Christ consciousness.

The right shade is the right choice or what she has been putting out. Removing the headphones is something she doesn't want to hear. She is searching for enlightenment by looking out the window. Lawnmower cutting the grass is cutting the old parts of self out. The people talking in here she can't hear because it no longer makes sense to her.

*****

The next few days continued to bring more information and insight for Patty and Ron.

"I see myself placed in a gold coffin to go from here to the other side. It is carried into my house in spirit world and placed over the bed.

Then the casket disappears and I am lying in bed. Next, I meet with Dad at a small round table by the bed.

After that I meet with a group of beings and answered questions. I hear someone say, "Once this starts it will escalate quickly".

The next day, September 5th, Patty had quite a long dream which spoke volumes.

"Ron and I go to this workshop seminar. Other people are there sitting at rectangular tables. He goes and sits on the opposite side from me at the end. It seems crowded so I don't go on that side. I sit at the end on this side and try to spread my things out from my backpack.

Then he gets up and goes to another table where there is more room.

A woman teaches the workshop.

I look for another more open table with room and there isn't any. I even open the closet door to see if there's a table in there but it's empty. I close the door.

I think, well there's nothing to learn here. I'll just leave. So, I gather my things and leave. I go out and there is Ron lying in a bed and he says, "Lie down with me a few minutes". He says something about the workshop and that he is ready to go. I say, "I wish I'd known that because I was ready to go a long time ago.

The workshop is about over and he says he'd like to just go talk to the teacher. I don't want to but say, "If you want to, okay, go ahead".

We leave and get in the car. Ron pulls out and follows other cars down a hill that is snow covered and slushy. We get to the bottom and need to get the address to see where we are.

We're in a house with two other males. I ask the address and he says, 'Palisades" (protection, fence, and barrier). I say I need the number and he says, Palisades. We go outside and I see someone and ask the address and he says 13609 or 13809.

We're walking and Ron pulls keys out of his pocket and says, "I think I know what happened. When I dropped the guard off, I gave him the other keys".

I said, "Were they Chevy keys?" He said, "Yes".

"I could see how it happened."

*****

This dream deals with the lesson we're in together and separation. (Going from the opposite of the table to another room and another table). The seminar is something I need to learn and incorporate; a learning experience we've gone through together. Backpack is the things I'm still carrying around.

Ron going to another table and spreading things out shows he's been thinking about how to spread things out.

No table and empty closet is nothing left and nothing for me to learn. The bed is the bridge between the unconscious and conscious. Ron is the conscious me speaking through the unconscious. I'm ready to leave and have been for some time.

Ron wants to talk to the teacher, something to learn. Snow is the symbol of latent truth; truth is there but hasn't been seen.

The address works out to a number 32 in numerology, karmic liberation. Keys are inner awareness that opens the door to all truth. Chevy is 27 in numerology, the energy that dissolves all duality.

*****

For some unknown reason, September did not bring any higher teachings. The only transcription came the end of the month, but that will come later. Patty feels they aren't finished but is unsure what is happening.

The next night, September 6th gave Patty an unforgettable experience.

'During the night, a being dressed in a long purple, gold and blue robe came for me. The robe is filled with jewels and he has long white hair. He wraps the robe around me and the next thing I know, we're walking down a street.

I ask, "What is this place?"

"The Magic City and this is all you're remember of this part of your journey".

The amazement Patty felt after this experience was too indescribable to put into words!

*****

The meditations continued to be deep and profound, providing even more experiences such as on September 22, 2011.

"I go into meditation with prayer and see Dad, Mom, my grandmother and Doug, an old friend. There are five gold doors in front of me. I open the middle door, number three and go through to the other side.

I am standing in front of my house in spirit world. They show me a split moving screen. The left side is in here and the right side is spirit world. I can see both at the same time. In front of my house is a calendar with the month of October at the top. The rest is blank.

Dad shows up and we begin walking down the street. There are beautiful trees in fall colors. I can feel the breeze on my face. Most of the trees are full of colored leaves and a few are on the ground. It is so beautiful. Dad tells me that he knows how difficult this seems for me but it's time to acknowledge what we both know is truth.

He takes me to my doctor visit. I can see me in the room talking to the doctor while Dad and I watch. There are two doctors in spirit world present as well.

Dad says, "You seek to promote the truth and here is your opportunity. Don't miss it. There will be tests to prove what you and Ron both already know. It's time for the two of you to walk the path you laid out before you."

Then Dad takes me to a room and I sit at a table. I see the recorder sitting in a corner. Three beings come into the room. Their light is pure gold and I feel so humbled in their presence. I also physically feel nauseated.

They are taking an inventory of me without me saying or thinking anything. When they are finished they leave.

From here the meditation goes even deeper and I am unable to bring any more back.

*****

There are so many emotions running through Patty; it was difficult to keep track of them. Then on September 25th, Patty received the following spirit communication from her dad.

"Hi princess, we love you both very much. I know you feel as though you've been on a roller coaster ride but that is about to come to an end.

The next week or so will see you both experience a great deal of acceptance. It's been hard on you both to go back and forth. Once that ends you will find yourselves actually feeling a sense of peace.

We are with you both and will help in any way we can. As you both know, meditation goes a long way in helping you through this process. The more you can do, the better, but please manage at least a half hour every day. No more procrastinating here, please. I promise it will help a great deal and you'll feel better. Enough said there.

Continue your work and communicating with each other. You are both experiencing many emotions. Don't go through it alone. Do it together. This is a special time for you both so share it all. You will find many gifts as you do.

Remember there is a time for everything. We're all here for you. Love, Dad"

*****

The roller coaster was exactly what Patty had been experiencing. Then just as they were going to sleep on the 27th of September, Patty saw the Anubis between her and Ron.

Anubis is the God of the afterlife, and thus it continues . . .

Chapter 22

It was difficult to believe it was the month of October. In Florida that's a beautiful time of year. All the flowers are in bloom, the humidity is gone and its glorious sunny days with blue skies and puffy clouds.

For Patty, there hadn't been any teachings come in and she wondered when they would continue. Still she was presented with dreams and meditations which offered more information.

Her dream on October 1, 2011 dealt with the fact that she was letting go of the earth plane and there was a celebration taking place over in spirit world.

"There are two couples and me. We finished something and they want me to go out with them. I think I'm not going to be the fifth wheel. They say at 5:30 they found someone to go with me. A man with white hair shows up. I said, "You waited until 5:30 to get someone, well, I'm not going out with you; I will go out with you but not with them".

We leave to go to this place. We share a pitcher of beer. We have to stay upstairs because you can only go downstairs if you graduated from Catholic High School."

The dream shows me leaving earth and I go to celebrate and have a pitcher of beer with someone from spirit world.

*****

Often time's things may just be shown to us as a quick flash of something. That has happened numerous times to Patty. On October 4th, just as she was waking up, someone showed her number 76. Number 76 deals with the end of an individual's karma.

The next day, Patty saw her primary doctor. She said there is definitely something going on and she referred her to a gastroenterologist. She said Patty would need a colonoscopy or it could be a constricted esophagus.

Well, waking up the next day, the roller coaster started running again. It was just how she felt when she woke up. She talked to Ron and he told her that his dreams this week all indicated she was leaving.

*****

That same day she received the following channeling which actually talked about some of Patty's feelings and what she was going through...

"We wish to continue our previous discussions as well as to acknowledge what you are experiencing on various levels.

There comes a period with each soul of both discovery and doubt. As they begin to see changes both in their physical realm and other realms, the stages of doubt and acceptance begin to materialize.

Their physical aspects speak to them through various symptoms within the physical body. The soul aspects speak to them on a much more elevated level. Yet periods of doubt continue to present themselves. One day they doubt any part of what goes on; yet the next day they accept it all without any doubt whatsoever. And thus, the battle continues. Again, this is merely part of the process.

As the experience continues there is more acceptance and less doubt until the doubt no longer is present.

Understanding the process and what is experienced makes the transition easier and smoother for all concerned. Remember that the soul knows exactly the truth of all that is experienced.

You have been experiencing what we have just talked about. The last week has seen an escalation in your physical symptoms. This will continue to increase at a more rapid rate. Time will acknowledge what we describe and your doubt will disappear.

The tests will provide the truth you both seek and there will be decisions for you to make so be ready. You both have the courage to endure what is coming.

You have nothing to worry about so please stop creating any; it is useless and only gets in the way of progress necessary for you both.

You are servants of the Almighty. Have you not always been provided for far better than you could imagine? Then, please no more worries.

Your focus is on what yet needs to be accomplished. Things will ease up with regard to Ron's mom. You will find you'll have more time for each other.

Once you see the truth and confirmation you both seek, you will each find your peace that is needed. There have been many tests and trials for each of you over these past years. It was all necessary and you have done well through it all. You have learned and prospered a great deal. We are thrilled with what you have realized.

Instead of jumping into something, you now take time and let it come in to realization. This was a big step for each of you. There were tricks along the way that you needed to experience. But the results were far worth it.

The result is a much higher level of existence than could otherwise be experienced. Now you can understand why it was necessary. Each of you now chooses the route of the soul instead of the ego.

You have let go of the many ideas of mass consciousness. In order to do this, much isolation was necessary. For both of you, the opinion of others was important and that no longer exists.

The rest of your journey will be smooth. You need only to enjoy your time left. Don't waste energy through worry, please. Instead spend the time appreciating and loving all that surrounds you.

Today you will begin to find the remaining answers you seek. We are proud of you both.

Council of All"

*****

Who Am I ...... Really?

Patty's next meditation on October 6th was quite enlightening.

"Dad and another being are waiting for me. We begin to walk down a street and come to a movie theater. I look up and see "This is Your Life" on the marquis.

We go inside and sit down. The movie is of my life. I see myself as a little baby sitting on Dad's lap. Then it goes to me as a toddler. Next, I am on the living room floor with our cat and dog. After that I'm shown a special Christmas when I get a doll's highchair and a Chatty Kathy doll.

From there we go to fifth grade and my crush on a schoolmate, then on to high school, meeting my high school love, prom and graduation.

After that I am going off to community college, then onto a girl's school for a year and finally to Ohio University. There I met four men I hung out with before marrying one of them.

I see the births of all my children and watch them grow up. From there I see my exit from Ohio, attending seminary school, meeting Ron, our relationship, marriage and all the places we traveled to both in the U. S. and Canada. Finally, it shows Florida and our life here.

The movie ends and when they role the credits, I see, Patty Stephens Plonski Kenner, born on May 20th and passed onto spirit world on ... and I couldn't see the date."

*****

This was quite a meditation looking back on all these parts of Patty's life.

Yet, the next day brought another indicator that came from a brief dream. She dreamt that Ron had tussled the top of her head and said, "I know the exact date when you're leaving." "When?" she asked, but he wouldn't tell me.

The dreams continued to tell Patty she is finished. Her dream on October 11, 2011 was graduation day. I'm in the auditorium and it's full of people. My brother comes and is waiting for me when I get out. There is an assembly. I get to leave early because I graduated.

I'm outside and my brother sees me and comes over to give me a ride. I think I'll just go home with him. I say to someone that I think I have to work next week and then I realize I don't have a job because I just graduated."

This dream is telling me I'm finished, graduated and leaving.

*****

The next night, the 12th, Patty had a unique experience that was unforgettable.

"Last night a very special healer came and asked me to go with her. She took me to a very special place. It was a field full of beautiful flowers. First, they were yellow and then they changed to all assorted colors. When you walked in the field, they would move to the side so you couldn't squish them.

I became a little girl about five years old and I sat in the field. When I did, the flowers moved around me and tickled me. There were butterflies everywhere.

I was giggling and laughing like a little girl. This was an actual experience over in spirit world.

*****

On the morning of the 14th, Ron told Patty that last night he had a dream where she was with him and a lawyer. The lawyer was ironing out all the details of her leaving and typing up loose ends. Ron got upset and walked out. When he came back she was just standing there feeling extremely sad.

Needless to say this day was quite shocking to say the least. No matter how much has been received about Patty leaving-it still seems astounding.

As if that weren't enough, Ron has been receiving various channeling from other people who also spoke of the fact that Patty was leaving. These were people who didn't even know her!

Chapter 23

Remember the bucket list I mentioned? Patty began her list today, the 14th of October 2011. The first item on her list is to eat fresh lobster. Ron took her out for dinner. She had a Maine lobster at Big Al's. It was wonderful. They sat and talked about spirit world, their love and communion. After that they went shopping and stopped for a wonderful decadent dessert.

This man loves Patty so very much and she loves him with all her heart. They have opened and shared their hearts in love. Never before has Patty been so cherished and she is grateful.

*****

On October 20, 2011, Patty received the following channeled message.

"What we have provided is truth for all. Your journey is complete and you have done well. Only a few more steps are necessary and you shall fulfill your destiny.

We do see your doubt and conflicting emotions yet you move forward and continue. Soon you will have the peace and understanding you seek.

For each soul, the journey is different yet many similarities do exist. We are with you and Ron every step of the way. The support you have with you is as infinite as the universe.

Today will provide you with many, though not all answers. You will each find your moment of acceptance within all that is revealed.

You need not worry that you were not being provided truth. It was always there, present in many forms from your intuition to your denial. Remember the stronger the denial, the more truth that exists within that denial. It is "the nail being hit on the head" so to speak.

We honor you always as you honor the Living God. All reigns within you. Many will be with you both today. Have no fear or worry. Your destiny is at hand. Trust, believe, all is well...Enoch"

*****

Although October was not a very busy month, the meditations and dreams continued. On October 3, Patty had a brief meditation.

"The first hour I was zoned out. Then Dad appeared and showed me 5 gears connected. He said, "All must be in place for it to move. Only one more piece and then it will move.

Then I see my house in spirit world and there is a huge bouquet of balloons out front on the mailbox. The front door is open and people are inside celebrating."

*****

Still everything keeps right on pointing to Patty leaving. What is amazing is just how many ways the universe will use to get the information to be realized. Talk about creativity! Between all their dreams and meditations, it's an enormous amount of insight. Patty just keeps being amazed at what she sees and experiences.

On October 30, 2011, Patty had the following meditation dealing with a final exam.

"Dad is waiting for me. I have on a white iridescent garment. I go up one escalator and he is waiting at the top. Together we go up five more flights to Level 6. We get off and he is beside me. Four beings appear and surround us, in front, back and on each side.

Next, I am in a room where I take my final exam. It is six pages long. Later I see A+ at the top of the page.

I am now in a hospital for a treatment. Mom is in her nurse's uniform. There is a gold liquid in an IV bag flowing in me. I see my relatives there.

Also, the recorder is there with my book of life. The last page has "The End" written in it. There are a few blank pates left. I ask, "How many pages are left?"

"Ten pages left".

After that I see something with "Final Destination" and a gold seal on it.

Ron is in a room behind a table and teaching a class. There are many people in there, some I know, some I don't".

*****

For Patty, the month of November seems to be filled with more dreams that are relative to the events she is experiencing. Her dream on November 2, 2011 showed another possibility of the job she might have in spirit world.

"I'm driving a bus of school children. There are two busses filled with children. I think we're on a field trip. Over the radio the other bus driver tells me the animals are out. There are animals blocking where I need to drive. I get out of the bus and help lead horses. There are huge tigers being lead on leashes. Two tigers start fighting. I think one kills the other.

I'm leading a horse and a man is leading a tiger and coming right toward me. The horse is jumpy and I manage to calm him. I'm afraid but know not to show fear or the tiger will attack. I walk by the other tiger without any incident.

School bus means I'm about to venture on an important life journey. The driver is the one in control. Horse is strong physical force and I'm leading him which means I'm in control of my energy. The radio is communication from guidance, message from my higher self. The tiger is a go getter and great strength and power of overcoming.

This dream deals with picking up souls in here and transporting them in spirit world. The animals represent people in here.

*****

Dreams not only provide us with information. They also show us what we hang onto from the past. Since Patty's dad had died when she was just nine years old, she never had the opportunity to say goodbye to him or to really grieve his leaving. She has been holding onto that energy for almost fifty years.

This next dream provided her the opportunity to say goodbye. It came on November 5, 2011.

"I am here to go through the process of Dad dying. It is a hospital where people are all dying. They have moved Dad to the final ward.

I walk into the room. There are about 7 beds on each side of the room. He is in the bed on the far-right side. I walk up to the bed. As I get near the end, it looks like there is a body and clothes are on the floor. I'm scared so I walk out.

I'm afraid to go back in because I don't want to step on the body, so I ask for help, someone to go with me (guide). It turns out there was just a pile of clothes on the floor. I remember a woman patient out of bed and walking as I went by her. There are lots of beds with people all dying. It's very difficult.

Dad just has a white sheet over him and a tube up his nose. I think he's unconscious. I tell him how much I love him. He wakes up and reaches out to put his arm around me. He says, "I love you too sweetheart, with all my heart", and then he dies."

*****

Needless to say, after this dream Patty did a great deal of crying and releasing. All this energy she had been carrying she could finally let go. It certainly was a catharsis!

Her next meditation on November 8, 2011 made quite an impact as well as providing her a healing. Before she began the meditation, she felt really nauseated. The first half hour she had burning pain from her right shoulder through the right side of her chest and arm. It was scary.

"Three angels come and get me. They surround me and the next thing I know we're going through a thick grey ty[e of veil to the other side.

They help me to go through it. When we get to the other side, I first notice a tremendous clarity I have not experienced before. Everything in and around me is crystal clear.

I am taken to a building and am in a processing center. There are papers that are stamped with a gold seal. They said, 'Step 4 completed November 2, 2011."

I see myself in the picnic area where I meet Dad. Mom came with him and she will help me go through stuff. (In the 2nd part of the tape, the pain starts to diminish).

The angels are always with me. When we come back in here it is through a tunnel. I could not come back through the veil. It is one way.

I am brought out early to write this and am told not to get up yet. Applesauce will help settle my stomach."

*****

Then on the morning of November 9, 2011, Patty was organizing the material for her book. Ron came in to talk. He looked at her and said, "Your aura is gold". Patty glanced at the clock and it was 9:29. As he looked at her, right over the top of her head it was deep purple. Out from that her aura was gold. How astonishing is that?

That same night Patty had one of those amazing dreams that actually was an experience.

"I remember seeing Dad and then three angels came for me. I am taken into spirit world to learn more about it. As we move through space, it is as if they are talking to me but instead of hearing their voices outside, I am hearing them from the inside.

When I have a question, I only need to think it and they answer. This applies to all souls.

It is explained that I have advanced up the ladder due to all my years of meditation and study. In a case where a soul is preparing to leave the earth plane, a great many others help with the education needed for departure. For many, most instruction and learning is provided while they are in spirit world.

As a human, many beliefs and philosophies exist which are not necessarily truth. Only when a soul seeks truth is it provided. When they are embellished within their own beliefs, without question that is where they stay.

Over time they begin to question their belief structure and only then does real truth present itself. Nothing is forced yet it is always available for growth and advancement.

Then I am taken to a huge hall of learning. Within the fluid walls, all is available for those who wish to continue their education. I am taken to a small room. Inside is a table and chair. The walls are covered in books from the floor to the ceiling. There are the books of all my lives. I am allowed to read any that I wish. The books have gold numbers that correspond to the numbers a soul needs to free themselves from the wheel of reincarnation.

As I look at the shelves I see the number 119. That is the book I wish to read. It is placed open on the table for me. As I absorb what exists within the pages I am told I am not able to bring this knowledge back into the conscious state. This is so that the rest of this journey would not be influenced by what I read. It all exists within my soul, including my time of exit. Knowing too much can influence too many aspects through my personality. I am told, 'Freedom is at hand yet you must secure it on your own. We anxiously await your arrival.

When I finish, we leave and once again travel back to the physical plane and I return to my bed. The angels hover over me. Just before they leave, I am given a gift. It is a gold heart. As I hold it in my hand, it becomes a beautiful eagle with huge talons. As he rests on my hand he turns to gold and I am humbled. I show them my love and gratitude and they are gone.

Each day, each moment, each breath provides us with a mirage of opportunities. It is up to us to find them and experience all we can realize.

*****

On November 9, 2011, Patty did some writing..." As I write this I have come to realize the changes occurring. Since yesterday the writings now occur in the early morning. Often, I feel I have no memory of the night before. Yet as I pick up the pen, all is provided. The three angels, called the "Angels of Transition" are now with me always. From here on out is for me to journal all I can both for myself and for others. It is available for all souls seeking truth."

Chapter 24

Another incredible experience came through in Patty's meditation on November 10, 2011.

"I start down the stairs and at the bottom is a wizard with his cape open. He wraps me in his cape. The next thing I know, someone yanks me out of there. (Somewhere I was not supposed to be so my protectors took care of it.)

I am put on a gold escalator and Dad is waiting for me at the top. We start walking and the floors are white marble.

Ahead of us are two huge gold doors that open toward us as we approach them. We go inside and I hear someone say, "Master Enoch is waiting". We are in a place and he comes toward me and extends out his hand. He has a gold ring on his finger with a huge blue stone in it. He says, "Will you walk with me?" "Of course".

Then we are outside in nature and end up sitting on the grass by a beautiful stream. The water is crystal clear and the sounds coming from the stream are musical. I can see fish moving and other animals around us.

He said he has some things to show me. He waves his hand over the stream and it is as if I am looking at my relatives interacting in their house. Then he waves his hand again and they are gone. He once again waves his hand and the scene is very bleak, grey with trees charred and burnt; the ground is charred as if no life exists. He waves his hand again and says it is time to go.

The next thing he says is that someone else is waiting for me. We go into a place with a full glass wall. A being comes toward me with the most incredible energy. His aura is gold and the light emanating from him is gold. I bow as he reaches for my hand. "I am called Arturius", he says. He takes me toward the window and shows me a gold book. In it are names. I only saw some of them, all former presidents, and he shows me my name and Ron's name in this book. I don't know what else was said but I know how important it is. The light everywhere is gold.

It is time to go and I am back with Enoch. I ask if I can go to my house. In a blink, I am there. I go through the house and out in the garden. I break down and start sobbing, saying "This is my home!" Then Mom and my grandmother show up. I am so happy to see them and can't stop crying... When I calm down it is time for them to leave. They go across a small bridge that is over a stream and wave goodbye.

I go back through the house and Dad is sitting on the steps waiting for me. I sit beside him and cry some more. Then it is time to go and he brings me back.

*****

When Patty came out of this meditation, she kept on releasing through her tears. This meditation was so powerful it is difficult to express in words. For this kind of experience, there are no adequate words! Each of these experiences seems to be even more profound than the one before. What more could there be?

Many times, we can meditate and not have conscious recall to bring it back. This can occur for several reasons. It can be we're very tired and end up falling asleep, or it may be blocked because we are not allowed to bring it back into a conscious state. It happens because the timing may not be right, or simply that it is too much truth and we couldn't handle it. So, it can be stored within the memory to surface at a later time.

The next meditation was quite strange for Patty, yet it still offered profound insight. It occurred on November 18th.

"I go up a gold escalator and Dad is at the top. There is a gold Rolls Royce car. He opens the door and I get inside. Mom, my grandmothers and aunts are there.

Ahead of us two huge gold doors open and we drive through them. We are driving out in the countryside and everything is so lush. I see white gates up ahead. They open outward and we drive through them. I realize it is a cemetery but there is only green grass and some flowers, no tombstones at all.

We pull up to a particular spot and get out there. There is a silver coffin ahead of us. I know it is mine. Everyone is celebrating and I feel this is symbolic.

We get back in the car and I find myself outside in nature by a stream. Jesus shows up and says, "Soon you will be coming home. We are preparing you for the journey. Then he leaves and Enoch shows up by the stream.

He waves his hand over the stream and I see my gastroenterologist looking at an x-ray on the wall. There is a grey shadow on the left side of the x-ray. He waves his hand again and it disappears.

I find myself in a room with the recorder and my book of life. He says there are ten pages left to be written.

Next, I am in my house and there is a huge dining room with a large table in it. It is filled with food and there are people everywhere celebrating. A huge turkey and every thanksgiving dish imaginable are on the table along with all kinds of desserts.

I go outside and sit on a bench with Dad. I don't recall what was said and from here I zone out. Throughout the meditation my stomach hurt on both sides and across the top".

*****

Patty's next channeling came on November 16, 2011 in order to let her know what was happening in and around her.

"Good day. Once again, we continue our discussions. Today marks a new level of understanding regarding what will occur in your future.

You will notice energetic changes which will occur in and around you. They will start with subtle changes and become more profound in time. It is important to document all that you can so carry the necessary tools with you.

Who Am I...... Really?

Also, you will find your own energy pattern changing. As your energy continues to shift out of the earth plane density, you will feel the shift more each day. Your physical energy depleting will cause more fatigue of the physical body. Yet although this will occur; your psychic energy will become more acute. You will find this avenue will open to greater understanding and awareness.

Today will allow you a greater acceptance of what occurs. Both of you have passed a hurdle so to speak.

You will have a need to take things slower yet there is more than sufficient time to complete what you wish to accomplish. Be open today in all avenues for the answers you seek will be provided. Trust in the divine and your heavenly father.

Council of 7"

*****

Then on November 19, 2011 a visit from Patty's Dad brought more insight.

"Hi Princess-we're all here tonight. Your journeys at night will escalate. There are things that need to be started. We'd like you to start writing some of your letters to those you wish to say goodbye. It's time. It will take a good while for you to complete them. So, think about who you want to write to and what to say. Bring closure to all that you can. There are some unsaid words that need to come out.

Next week is the time to put the final organization to the book. Then together we'll write, probably toward the end of next week. Things will begin to slow down for you physically. I know you're already beginning to feel it.

You'll find the periods of rest will provide some energy bursts so use it when you need it.

Your sleep will become more broken. The time for sleeping will begin to change. You may be awake more during the night and find more need to sleep during the day. Adjust where you need it.

We're working with Ron as far as preparation. I know you want to make it as easy for him as you can. We'll help where we can.

Please get out for some fun while you're able. You're going to find that time frame short lived. So, plan what you really want to do. Go through things as you can to get rid of what you don't need. Find simple ways to have fun. It will go a long way.

We are all so proud of both of you, all you've accomplished and what is yet to be completed. You are both special to so many here. We all love you...Dad"

*****

Again, two days later Patty's Dad came in on the 21st. "Hi Princess - I just wanted to touch base with you. Everything is moving forward in preparation for your arrival. Please work each day you can. It is vital and necessary for the energy to begin.

There was a lull so we could get things in place here. Now is the time and the energy is moving once again.

The two of you are ready and have reached an understanding on five out of seven levels. You have all seven levels, Ron has five. You each have a job to do both individually and collectively. The love you share and offer will sustain you through it all.

Your soul's connection merely grows and deepens each moment of each day. It is very special to many. That's all for now. We love you very much...Dad"

*****

Then on November 23, 2011, Patty had a dream which actually showed the connection she and Ron would share. He would be doing the work from the earth plane while she would be his new connection to spirit world.

"Ron and I are at seminary school. We are part of a ceremony. A woman who started us there ran the ceremony. There are seven of us. We're on stage. Ron goes first and kneels down. Then I go and kneel down. Later she says, "I have a question. Why don't you come and work in the kitchen?"

"I'm having a lot of health issues", I said. Ron looks at me and wants to say why we really don't come.

The next morning, we show up. We have three coolers. Ron takes the cooler on wheels that looks like a red wagon. I carry a large white cooler by the two handles. We go inside and I say, "Upstairs or down?"

"Downstairs", he says. I carry the cooler downstairs. One small white cooler is outside beside the car".

*****

The ceremony is initiation, graduation. Number seven is completion. The stage is where we work with spirit. The next morning is new beginnings. Three coolers keep the situation on hold. The red wagon is childlike, lighthearted. I'm carrying the white cooler. This cooler is the work I'll do from the other side. Two handles, is the control of the situation. The one small cooler left by the car is the work Ron will do from this side.

On November 29, 2011 Patty had a dream which showed her what purgatory is all about. "I'm in a place where people thought they were on vacation. It's run by a group who has control over everyone. We're outside. You weren't allowed to call anyone by name but I asked if a guy could call about his shoes. That was okay to do.

People are walking and trying not to be noticed or picked up. I run into another girl and she says, "Don't use real names when calling. Call someone by another name". "Okay, Judy", I said. It was the first name that came to mind.

People just didn't know what was going to happen to them. Strange looking vehicles were driving around trying to pick up people. Everyone just wanted to leave any way possible."

In this dream, I was in purgatory, where people go to work things out before they can move on. There was a sense of fear among everyone. I had no fear. I knew I was just visiting and to help. It was a very grey place.

*****

The very last day of November gave Patty a short meditation. "Dad is on top of an elephant and he tells me to climb on top. There is a cellophane type covering over a doorway to the other side. I merely push it aside and we go through it.

I see or hear the recorder say I have eight pages left to write in my book of life.

A row of gold orbs surrounds me from top to bottom. Then I see myself in my house in spirit world sitting on a chaise in the sunroom. I have a book in one hand and a drink in the other."

Chapter 25

December was the month Patty originally thought she would be leaving. Yet somewhere in October she woke up one morning and knew something had changed. She really felt she wasn't going anywhere for a while.

Then as she began the book; she knew she couldn't leave until it was written. This was the last project she needed to finish in this life. So, December continued with the dreams, meditations and teachings.

On December 2, 2011 Patty had the following dream. "I wrote a check to pay for two tickets for $55.00. Someone (guide) told me I'm not responsible for anyone else, just myself.

So, I said, 'I'll cancel it and only pay $33.00 for one ticket". Number 33 is the master of the spiritual.

Patty and Ron still feel they are on a roller coaster ride that is never ending. On December 5th, Patty's Dad brought through a channeling.

"Hi Princess, thanks for the doorway. We all know what you and Ron are feeling and experiencing. If we could make a few observations and suggestions.

First, the more you talk, express and communicate, the better you both will feel. Just discussing in honesty brings you each closer while removing the barriers you may think you need for survival. You don't need the barriers; it's merely your perception. Being open is your key, for both of you!

Now, just a simple suggestion. Instead of letting things churn and roll around inside, why not express what you're experiencing. Of course, you feel vulnerable. But we promise it's a better outcome to express than to withhold what is going on. So, please try it instead of waiting until it wants to explode.

Now about the wavering and we're speaking to you both in several areas. First you, princess, but it also applies to both of you. There is no going back! Let me emphasize this again. THERE IS NO GOING BACK!

Look at what you've written, channeled and experienced over the last three years both physically and spiritually. There is no denying what is occurring and has occurred on so many levels. I know you want things put in order with proof and dates and anything else you can think of but it just doesn't work that way! Even the energy you use when you waver has an impact on the whole. So, please realize where you are, where you've come from and where you must go.

Okay, now onto my favorite son, "For God's sake, PLEASE stop your wavering and even more so, your worrying!! It serves no purpose other than mucking things up. If you keep it up you'll end up in quicksand.

Now for some straight points just to remind you! 1. You have always been taken care of and provided for in a far better way than you could have imagined. 2. You are a spiritual warrior. You have a mission and it must be completed. You asked for it, you agreed to it so let's get on with it. 3. What you question about seminary school will happen. You only must be open. Don't jump, don't do anything. We will bring it in when it's time. Just be open. 4. Just for now, live life with Patty. Each moment is a gift. Live your love to the fullest each moment of each day. Please, you both need it. 5. Lastly, the other woman coming in after Patty leaves; we only ask you to be open again. The events and experiences will be brought to you as needed. Just quit the worrying and be open.

Well, for now I've said enough. The tone was what was needed and said with the greatest love of all... Mom and Dad"

*****

On December 6, another incredible experience happened in Patty's meditation. "Enoch came to get me and three angels are with him. I am wearing a white and gold garment. We all begin to levitate through layers. I look up and notice a white and gold cover over us. I ask why it is there. I am told it is only for now when I'm still on the earth plane so we can travel to the upper levels. Once I cross over it won't be needed.

I find us standing in front of my house. I see "Congratulations" signs on our way there. We stand looking at the house when all of a sudden it turns to little sparkling lights and just disintegrates to the ground. I am shocked!

They just smile at the shock and disbelief on my face and say, "that really wasn't needed. It was there for as long as you needed it to be". I am impressed that I would be here to recoup my energy and heal but for a very short time.

Next, they take me to meet with a very high level being who merely is called, "The I AM the ALL". Jesus takes me there. We discuss what I'll be doing once I get there.

He holds out his hand. As I look in the palm, I can see buildings and souls inside these buildings. He says they all had a mission. I ask for information and what I would be doing.

He told me it wasn't time yet for it to be revealed so I would not be able to bring it back. I felt so happy at seeing what I would be doing. From here I zone out. I am told I have six pages left to write in my book of life."

*****

Then, on December 7, 2011, Patty had the following dream. 'Ron and I are outside waiting to get tickets. There are other people there. We're sitting on a bench. I feel mucus in my throat. I reach in and start to pull it out. I pull out this long thick cordlike growth and toss it to the ground. It is tinged with blood. Ron gets upset and says, "Oh that came out of you!"

This dream dealt with all the things that were unexpressed through the years. Patty has finally dealt with her past and now expressed through communication. So, this "growth" was all that energy coming out.

The same day, Patty had another meditation showing her being liberated from all the tests and karma here in the natural world.

"Someone handed me a golden ticket. It is number 128. A silver train comes and I get on it and my ticket is punched. The train pulls into where it is a processing center. It is like a wheel with spokes coming out of it. Then I am with many other souls and we are walking down a long hallway. When we get to the end of the hallway, I go through a turn style and someone takes my ticket.

Later I see myself dressed in a white and gold garment with jewels. A beautiful crown is placed on my head. It is very heavy and full of jewels in all colors. I am seated at an altar. There are 24 beings also there.

As I began this journey, an owl was on my right shoulder and an eagle was on my left shoulder. During the journey, they both turned to gold. Then I zoned out."

Number 128 is equal to 32 x 4. Number 32 is liberation from all karma and tests here in the natural world.

*****

That night when Patty and Ron went to sleep, she had the most unusual experience.

"Just as we were to go to sleep I saw Enoch, dad and the woman who would come into Ron's life after I'm gone., I was quite shocked. She asked if she could speak to me and I said, "Yes, just wait till I go to sleep and am out of my body."

She was very humble and wanted to know if I was all right about her coming in to have a relationship with Ron. I told her I was more than okay with it. I told her I want Ron to be happy. I know he really needs to be with someone and it's necessary for him to complete what he came in here to do. I thanked her for coming to talk to me, but it wasn't necessary. I love Ron and want what's best for him. I know she had many past lives with him, just as I have.

We are all soul mates. There is not one soul mate, there are many.

This is what I remember and thinking about it the next day, I realized what an incredible experience I had been given. How many other women would understand that first of all, when they died there was another one coming right in, and two, how many would be able to handle it?

What issue comes in is that as we grow up we are taught there is only one person we can love. Then when we marry them, we own them and they own us. This is one of the biggest illusions of all! There is no unconditional love here, merely the rules and conditions we place on love!"

*****

Then the following day, Patty had another meditation in which she was only able to bring back part of it. She realized that often it may be the universes' way of only giving us as much as we can handle.

"I am standing under a green streetlight. I look up and see a large owl. He came and told me to climb on his back. When I do I am now in the center of his wings and there are feathers that come up around me. We take off and I can see all the stars in the sky. We head toward one of them. There is a beautiful white gate and I can see it's open. We go inside and I am at some kind of reception where there are many people. There is a cake that says, "Welcome". It is a reception for me. Everyone is there to welcome me home.

Then Dad takes me into a building. I know it deals with the work I'll be doing. I can't recall what was being said. I know I wasn't asleep; I am just unable to bring anything back with me."

*****

On December 20th, Patty experienced a great deal of insight which came through a dream.

"I'm cooking a meal for many people. Ron thinks the vegetables are cooked too much. I say, "Not everyone can handle them crunchy like you can. This meal is for everyone. I have everything ready to serve but I am told I must wait until I receive number 137 silver."

137 is the four aspects of God,

1= #17 the soul in both worlds

2&3 = #50, all things holy

4= 333 mastering spiritual consciousness

137 is when the individual and cosmos are progressing in evolution side by side. Also, number 7 is in the bible 137 times.

So, after all this Patty has to wait for this silver ticket.

*****

On December 10, 2011 Patty had a channeling come through her writing. "Good day. Thank you for answering our call. We wish to provide you with more information.

Your final project is nearly ready to begin building. All information is nearly ready to transcribe. We have been preparing you at night and in your meditations. We will provide you ample time needed for completion.

Once you begin it will easily flow and you will be amazed at its development. It will speak to all souls on many levels from beginning to advanced. The energy of your words will help to activate energy within each soul. We will be with you each step of the way and many others will come through your vehicle from time to time.

Keep on logging as you have for a short while longer. For now, reflect through your material at hand. The writing shall be done in the space and energy we have provided. It has been nurtured for many months in preparation for what is to come.

We are pleased with the steps taken thus far. We shall move forward together to serve all mankind.

You have done well. Be open to our call and all will prevail. Your schedule is nearly complete. Until we meet again . . .

Peace,
Council of 7"

*****

On December 12, 2011, Patty had a dream that once again talks about spirit world. 'I'm helping someone move to a new place. Ron is with his mom. I call him to see what he's doing. "I'm cooking", he says. "What are you cooking?" "I'm cooking with olives". I said, "I appreciate you so much more and more".

I had walked across the porch to go inside. The porch is all bricks and I thought it was a great place to put plants."

Cooking is putting together many ingredients of life. Olive is healing and immortality. Porch is the part of self out in the open. Inside deals with self-introspection, some family issues for me to investigate. The red bricks are unsettled business, building new direction. Plants are spiritual development and growth.

This dream deals with my moving into a temporary building in spirit world in order to review my life.

*****

The next day what Patty experienced was another profound meditation that was astounding beyond words.

"I am going through a tunnel filled with purple and blue mist. At the end is a white light. I go up a gold escalator and Dad meets me at the top. I find myself wearing a navy blue business suit. Dad has on a blue silk suit that glistens and puts off a light that emanates a beautiful purple and gold color.

I am carrying a briefcase. "We have a meeting", Dad says. We start walking and I find myself in front of 7 beings, the Council of 7. They all emanate gold and white auras. I am asked questions and see myself using an easel to explain what I feel is related to the book.

Dad is off to the side and I see the recorder sitting in the corner. When I finish, he tells me there are four pages left in my book of life.

I then find myself in a beautiful garden where I am joined by a being who is "THE ALL". I am so humbled and kneel before this incredible presence. I have been here before and the experience is unforgettable. I know not what is discussed by just the presence goes far beyond any other encounter.

I leave here and thoughts start bouncing in my head. So, I take myself to a deeper level through breathing and counting.

The moment I do, I see myself in the most breathtaking gold gown with a long train. The garment radiates gold light and it is a living garment. I wear a gold crown on my head.

On each side of me are twelve beings who proceed with me down an aisle. Ahead is a gold throne. They seat me in the throne. Above me is a huge gold bong. I hear, "The seven seals are open". Then the bong is struck seven times. Each time it is struck, there is a beautiful gold energy that goes through me like nothing ever experienced before.

When it is completed I hear, "The light body is illumined". Now I am totally energy free of physical attachment of any kind.

I feel someone with me giving instructions. They have me move through rooms in our condo, even finding Ron and playing with his hair. They have me practice going through the walls of the room and going down to the condo below. I am told to go through the wall and outside. I do an am hovering outside, just above the lake. When I first go outside my balance feels wobbly.

They bring me back in and have me practice going in and out of my physical body lying on the bed. After five in and out moves, I am quite nauseated so they bring me out. I have astral traveled for years, still this is unlike anything I've ever experienced.

I give thanks for all these blessings."

*****

The same night, the 14th, Patty had quite a long-detailed dream that deals once again with her leaving.

"I'm at a place where there is a huge house. I have been outside and see a man dressed in a black priest's robe. He was looking at the house and property.

Ron calls me and says it's time to go. As I go inside I said, "Who is that man?" I wondered if he is a lawyer. I go upstairs to the top floor (3rd) to collect things to leave.

There are two women lying on a mattress on the floor. They are completely covered with a blanket so you can't see them, just hear them. They are laughing and talking.

I said, 'Sorry to interrupt but I have to get my things to leave". There are three things in a pile on the floor, two books and a sympathy card for mom that I was going to write."

The priest is a guide looking at the house, everything I've done. The phone call is communication, the guides trying to get my attention. It may be to confront an issue I'm avoiding. It's time to go, the end of something. Mattress is the bridge between the two worlds; I have new responsibilities that require my attention. There are three things, past, present and future.

This dream deals with my leaving. Instead of focusing on a date of departure and what I have to do, I need to get out and have fun.

Chapter 26

Patty often wondered how objects end up being manifested on earth. She's not talking about how they are made in a factory, or even how they are designed. She is talking about how things are created from that first spark of thought about an object.

Her next meditation on December 14, 2011 gave her some insight as to just how it all happens.

"A white unicorn picks me up. I climb on his back and we go through a tunnel filled with purple light. We come out the other side and there are three beings waiting for me. When they come into my energy it feels so strong. The bed I am meditating on (in the physical world) is really vibrating.

They take me into a building they call "Creation". We go into what appears to be a classroom. It is full of souls. It is explained that they are learning how to create by using energy to manifest into objects in spirit world.

Next, we go into another building where engineers create anything such as buildings, bridges, etc. that would then come through to the earth to be manifested there.

From here we go to a building where scientists meet to create what is necessary and then it comes through to the earth plane. I see diagrams and equations I could never begin to explain. Then I zone out . . .

Somewhere in this meditation someone hands me something on a spoon to swallow. It is yellowish gold in color. I open my mouth and closed my jaw and actually felt it in my physical body. Manna? I only know it was quite thick, very sweet with a very strange taste.

*****

Patty's next meditation on December 16, again spoke about the preparations being made for her leaving.

"I go through a tunnel filled with purple and gold light. Dad is waiting at the end of it. I am told to practice levitating and going through the wall and then outside. Then practice back and forth. I feel fine while I'm in the condo but once I go back and forth outside, I get very nauseous.

While I am outside, I feel such a difference in the energy. It is higher, more refined energy.

There is a guide nearby and I can hear his thoughts. I am told that this change in vibration will continue. When a soul prepares to exit the earth's energy, their vibration changes. As their vibration is elevated in preparation for departure, more and more of the lower dense vibration begins to dissipate.

Even though I have astral traveled for years, from here on out the astral travel becomes different in the nature of vibration. The more a soul prepares to leave the physical body, the more the cord connection begins to expand, therefore thinning.

Picture a thick rubber band that is being stretched out. As it stretches it begins to become thinner until it finally breaks. I am starting to feel the thinning of the cord.

Next, I am taken to a beautiful garden full of trees and flowers, all of which are in complete harmony. Here I meet with five beings; they are all writers who will be working to help me put the book together. I receive instructions on how to organize it. From here I zone out.

*****

Then a week later, on December 25, 2011 Patty received the following channeling through writing. "I am grateful to once again share our energies. We have traveled far and wide together, you and me, long before you knew of my existence. I have watched and participated as you grew and evolved like a beautiful flower opening from the beginning of time. Now you are in full bloom, every petal perfect and expanded out for all to see with the colors and aromas of the universe.

Your Father in heaven applauds deeply and anxiously awaits your arrival and celebration. Your work is nearly finished. Soon you will have the rest you need and so much more. Next week begins your final segment. We look forward to aiding you in this endeavor. God bless you ... Enoch"

*****

The next meditation which occurred on December 28, 2011 speaks for itself.

"There is a black and gold carriage waiting for me. The door opens and Dad is inside. I get in and the carriage turns gold. It is pulled by two white horses. We go through a purple mist and at the other end is a beautiful golden light.

From here I start to see flashes of past lives. One, I am wearing a purple velvet hat and dress. It takes place in England. I am of nobility. I see myself going into a huge mansion. I to up the stairs and into the bedroom. There a man who is my husband is in bed with two women. I carry a small gun in my purse. I take it out and kill myself. As the scene faces I ask who these people are in the present life. It turns out that I know them all.

Next, I am flying in a military plane that drops bombs. We fly over an ocean. I am the pilot. My plane is shot down and crashes into the water.

This was all I could bring back. Then I see a former president with Dad. They show me another building where healing takes place. It is explained that this is a very special place. The purpose is for souls who have been ill for a very long time, years, either physical or mental in nature. They may have been in a coma, have Alzheimer's or something similar. These souls need to be gently taken care of and to be brought through healing into their present situation.

Each soul response may be different. For some healing occurs more quickly than others. The healing energy here is like nothing I have ever experienced.

Then I zoned out and when it ends, I am unable to move. I can swallow but that is all. Finally, after about five minutes I try to open my eyes. I did but had to close them again. After another ten minutes, I can finally move."

*****

As if this wasn't astounding enough, another very strange experience happened to Patty on December 28, 2011, during her sleep.

"I am sound asleep. I am in very deep water. It is clear but at first dark around me. As I look up I can see a bright light. I know must hold my breath in order to make it to the top and fresh air. I'm not sure I can do it. It feels like my lungs can't hold the air any longer. The entire time I am just moving up toward the light.

Just when I think I can't hold my breath anymore I burst through the top of the water and gasp for air."

At this point I wake up gasping for air and coughing until I can catch my breath. It was so real and quite scary.

Ron thinks I was practicing leaving my body. The reason he knows is because that is exactly what his dad went through when he died. Even stranger is that Ron and I were talking about this experience in our kitchen. I hadn't yet written it down. Then I came back to the bedroom and wrote down the experience.

When I finished writing I went into the bathroom and began to read a few pages of the latest book I am reading. It talked about one character during the war where a bomb went off near him. All he remembered was *swimming up to the bright light.* Then he came back to life and a fellow soldier was doing CPR on him because his heart had stopped.

Talking to Ron and telling him about the experience, then reading about a similar experience all happened within a fifteen-minute period!!! Coincidence?? Makes you wonder, but I don't think so!

*****

Even more astounding experiences continued for Patty...the next one being on December 30, 2011.

"I fly through a tunnel filled with purple light. When I come out the end, Dad is waiting for me. I don't remember much after that until I am sitting on a bench and a biblical figure appears and asks me to go with him. I said, "I'm not able to recall much. Can you please take me somewhere?"

He told me there is a great deal I am unable to bring back but he said he would show me something special. In the blink of an eye we are in a place that looks like a magical playground. There are children everywhere, of all ages, even babies. He explains that this is where children come when they cross over. The energy is very special and magical. He said, "There is someone I want you to meet."

A young girl who looks to be about twenty comes toward us. I knew immediately who it was, my sister Ellen from when Mom had a miscarriage. I am thrilled to meet her. She told me that she loves it there so much that she stayed on to help with the care of the others.

The next thing I know the figure said, "Jesus wants to see you". In a blink, I am before him in a type of garden. I am so humbled. He takes my hand as I look into his eyes and feel this incredible love that knows no bounds. He thanks me and honors me for the work we are doing. He said, "Your journey here is nearly at an end." There is something about February 13th. I feel that's not when I'm leaving but maybe there would be more clarity that day."

Chapter 27

The month of January began with more and more insight. Patty was amazed at the events. Her meditation on January 1, 2012 began it all.

"I shoot through a tunnel to the other side. Dad is waiting. I meet with twelve elders to discuss what I have accomplished and my time left here on earth.

The woman who will be with Ron when I leave came to ask me if she could trust him. I told her he was the most sensitive and compassionate person I knew. I said, "Yes, you can trust him but he can also see through any facade."

After that I am in a forest and I see Ron's Black Panther totem animal. We walk to the end of the forest. He tells me we must say goodbye. Years ago Ron had shared him with me, as well as his elephant, for protection. I reach down and stroke the panther and said goodbye. We walk to the edge of the forest and he turns to go back into the forest as I continue forward. The elephant shall be with me for a time yet."

*****

These are amazing animals who appear whenever I am threatened or need any sort of protection. It is like having a very strong bodyguard!

Patty's next meditation on January 2nd involved glimpses of several past lives.

"I go through a tunnel and immediately go into a past life. It takes place in a ballroom that is very ornate in decor. There are three gentlemen that are actually vying for my attention. One is quite boisterous, one is very quiet and wants to stay in the background. The third one is quiet yet very strong in character and confident. All three of them also exist in my present life. The first is my ex-husband, the second is Ron and the third is my dad.

Dad is the one who succeeded. I ask who I am in that lifetime. I was Queen Isabella. It was 1817. I died a natural death in that life.

Later I am with a biblical figure. I see myself asleep in bed with Ron and I rise up out of my body and say goodbye to him. Then I leave.

I also see another scene. I am lying in bed. Ron is sitting beside me holding my hand and we say goodbye."

I don't know if either of these will happen but they were very real.

*****

January 4th brought several surprises for Patty. Several special visitors came in and channeled messages through here. Here are the channelings.

"Hello, my dear and thank you for this brief time. I wish to congratulate you for your accomplishments. Our Father in heaven is very pleased to have you return to the fold.

You too have served as I have and experienced many opportunities for continued growth. Often it is the simplest of souls who had the greatest impact on me.

I will journey again with you to our magical realm here. Again ,you will enter the heavens as a child.

Continue to cherish your days there with the souls you love and all you meet. There is little time left, so cherish each moment and breath.

M.T."

*****

Hello, Patty, it's good to share your energy one more time. I have watched the two of you over the years. Seeing your two hearts share as one has given me great joy. You each have walked with me in other lifetimes and all are special to me.

Both of you have greatly impacted the other in your growth and wisdom. You each have sacrificed yourselves to aid in the others maturity. I honor you for that.

Remember this, please. Ron could not complete his mission had you not been there to help. Neither could you complete your wheel of reincarnation had he not been there for you. All planned, all designed, yours completed and his soon to be executed for final completion. You each have done well my child.

I look forward to celebrating with you in love.

K.F.T."

*****

The next visit was from the ex-husband of the next woman coming to Ron.

"Hello Patty and thank you. I promise this won't hurt a bit. I know you have reservations but please trust what I have to say.

For Ron, this union deals with his own mission and its success. To go against it would mean failure. For her, it is a means to finish what she started in this lifetime.

You have taken Ron as far as you can. Yes, I'll repeat that. You have taken Ron as far as you can. You have laid the necessary groundwork and built a solid foundation that allows the rest to continue.

Now it's someone else's job to cross the finish line. You have done well and so has Ron. Help him to continue as well. Thanks for your time.

B."

Then another communication from Patty's Dad came in on January 6, 2012.

"Hi Princess. Well today sure is a big day for you both. We are all thrilled and proud of what you each have accomplished. You've both come a long way.

There is much I cannot reveal, but let me say this: You will have the confirmation of how you're leaving before it occurs. Rest assured there will be no doubt as to your technical reason for death. It has been in the works for some time. The fact that you have previous knowledge is what shall have such a major impact on the world. Many will question their own mortality and their mission in life.

It will cause a major shakeup for years to come. Many who sleep will be shaken awake. Many who hurt will find comfort and peace. The world will begin to change all because of the work you both have done.

Thank you, Ron and Patty. We send you all our live.

Dad"

*****

January 6th also provided an exciting new experience for patty. Ron had just come out of meditation. He had received a major healing.

Afterward he was lying on the bed telling Patty about it. As he talked she could see colors when he spoke. They came out of his mouth, purple, blue and gold. There were colors of his aura over his face. Patty had never experienced anything like that before.

So many different experiences to take in and process.

Then Patty had her usual meditation on January 7th only this time she felt she slept through the first half of the meditation. Then suddenly, she had recall again.

"A guide with long white hair comes for me. I ask if he would take me somewhere. We go to a processing center. He lets me stand behind a worker and watch as he is taking care of souls that just arrived back home. They have a kind of ticket that he takes from them. It is something that looks electronic. The worker scans the ticket to see where they will go. Do they need to be in a hospital for rejuvenation? It not, they will go on through processing and on to orientation.

During this time, I had some very sharp pains that occurred in my left breast. They are very sharp like a knife and each one lasts a few seconds."

*****

Patty's next meditation on January 9th dealt with saying goodbye to an old friend.

"I see a gold sphinx and a purple stone in the 3rd eye. I go inside and I'm out in the desert. As I begin walking there is a red river ahead of me. I cross it and my elephant is waiting for me. I climb on his back. His harness has jewels in it. He takes me to the edge of a forest where I climb off because I must say goodbye. I no longer need his protection. I thank him and rub on his trunk. He says we have traveled many lifetimes together.

After that a gold eagle comes for me to climb on his back and we soar through the universe. We move toward a very bright light. Next, there is a tropical pool of water that is liquid gold. A man sits on the bank by this pool. I go into the pool for cleansing.

A tiger is waiting when I climb out. The tiger turns white and I look between the tiger's eyes and there is a green stone and light. It then turns gold. My 3rd eye turns gold and is open.

Next, I am in a city of gold. There is a guide outside a building. It has a gold dome. We go inside and it's a church with all colored lights streaming through the glass windows. I kneel before the throne and colored lights flow through me.

Then it becomes a gold light flowing through me. I sit on the throne. There are 24 around me. They are to meet with me.

Only a few weeks left to get out and have some fun. My energy is waning. I need more sleep.

Dad and a crowd wave goodbye. They had all been watching. Doug, an old friend calls out, 'See you soon Patty".

*****

These meditations in themselves write their own story. With all the changes, Patty still feels her energy is very scattered in many directions.

Her next meditation on January 15th showed that the pages left to write in her book of life are dwindling.

"There is a gold door and I go through it. Dad is with me and I find myself once again in a beautiful garden with this high level being. I remember I can ask questions. Most of them I can't recall but I do remember the quickness of entering spirit world so easily. It is explained that there is no separation and with each meditation it becomes easier.

I spend time with my mom. It feels so good to be with her. I ask if it was all real about me leaving and she assures me it is real.

At some point, I am in a room and I remember seeing the recorder. I only have half a page left to finish my book of life. He tells me the book I'm writing should be completed by around February 23, 2012.

Also, I am shown a beautiful mansion in spirit world. It has a circular drive and in the center is a large gorgeous fountain. As the water flows I can hear musical notes. I go inside the mansion. I feel it is mine."

*****

The next meditation occurs on January 16th. Patty finds she again can ask questions, but that doesn't mean she'll receive the answers. Patty also is finding that as her energy depletes, she often finds she zoned out the first part of the tape. She wonders if she's just so tired, or is this on purpose.

"I zone out for most of the first half of the tape. Then a huge purple dragon comes for me. We fly to this mountain top. I can ask questions. I ask about my ultrasound and am told it's an enlarged lymph node. I ask where we go when I zone out and have no recall. I am told we go to a place and receive instructions that are not to be brought back to the conscious awareness. It is necessary with regard to the level of learning and development.

Next, I'm in spirit world and people are lined up on either side of a path. I must walk through the path and as I do they separate. They all congratulate me.

I am told I am beginning to see a clear picture of no time and space. Also, I talked to someone about the book.

Then I'm near a stream and there is a bridge across the stream. There are others with me who are new transitions. We are talking among ourselves.

A new guide, Thomas is with us. He tells me I have experienced a great deal more than others. Thomas brought me to this level to experience other souls who are not as mature as I am. I am humbled by his words.

He tells me there will come a time when I will help other souls. I then see myself speaking in what's called the "grand arena". It is like an outdoor coliseum and is full of souls. They are listening to what I say. I am wearing a white robe.

Then we go back to the higher levels. I am told there are five of us who will work together in the time to come. We are all masters. Once again, I am humbled.

It is nearly time to go and we must say goodbye.

I see Mom and Aunt Jean in the distance. They smile and wave. I can see easily into other levels. They cannot enter where I am but I feel their love."

Chapter 28

One thing Patty has come to realize is that whenever her mom shows up in her nurses' uniform, it means another healing. Patty's meditation on January 19th, 2012 was definitely one of those.

"Mom comes in her nurses' uniform. I had asked for a healing. I'm floating in the ocean lying on a yellow raft. I can feel the waves wash over me and the sun on my face. I don't have a care in the world.

In a blink, I'm taken to the stables. I brush my horse, saddle him and we take off on a trail through the woods. Riding, itself, is such a healing for me. I bring him back to the stables when I finish.

Now I'm in a room with a large conference table and huge leather chairs around it. Dad is there with someone who will be instrumental in getting the book off the ground. I am sitting across from them. Dad gets up and moves to my side of the table.

The woman is laying out the terms of the agreement, publishers and how it will be set up. She has the manuscript in front of her with a blue rubber band around it.

Ron walks in wearing a suit and tie. He goes to her side of the table and shakes hands with her. He sits down beside her and is briefed on everything.

All the paperwork has a gold seal on it. I can see many souls watching from above on the other side. It is as if they are seated in a circular gallery above us.

Ron and the woman get up to leave. I stay there with Dad. A gold book appears on the table. Dad tells me to quit worrying; it will all be okay.

We go to leave and a purple dragon comes for me. I climb on his back and we fly out among the stars. I can see the constellations, the bear, big and little dippers.

Then suddenly, I am seated on a gold throne and wearing a gold crown. There are 24 beings around me. I am there to take in the energy of the throne.

Now, I am out at my mansion and see the grandeur of it all. I stand outside in these huge gardens filled with every flower imaginable in every color. I am awestruck by not only the beauty but the perfect balance of it all.

I see an old friend trying to butt her way in and two guides holding her back. They take care of her.

A grey fox coming toward me. It changes to an Indian named Grey Fox. He says, "I am to journey with you. I stand by your side. I protect you." I thank him. He says, "Many try to interfere with your work. I keep them away".

I see huge angels in pink that surround me. I hear a loud voice say, "God protects his children".

Now I see a bear and an elephant. They turn to gold.

We approach a very shallow stream we must cross. Grey Fox leads me across the stones. This is the last stream to cross. He shows me other streams we have crossed that were very deep and says, "These are the emotions. This stream flows clear. We are all tested."

Ahead of me is a solid large gold ring standing upright. It must be twenty feet tall. It looks solid yet it's moving and alive. I approach it and know I must go inside it. When I do, it comes over me and surrounds me. It is *the eternal circle of life*. As I stand there it becomes a ring of fire around me. The fire then turns to a deep purple flame.

Now I'm lying on a bed. I have been given a healing, cleansing and purification. I am *One with the ALL*."

Once again, this meditation is quite profound. Patty is speechless!

*****

The purpose of a channeling that came on January 20, 2012, was to provide Patty and Ron more information about what was occurring on a physical level.

"Good day. We wish only a brief moment of your time in order to provide you with some vital information.

You are starting to feel the beginnings of soul energy transfer. Your experience yesterday solidified that fact. You will see and feel you have less energy to utilize while you work.

Ron will see your experience and aid you in deciding where and who you place your energy around.

It is time to recognize the obvious. Try to work in two hour increments then take a break. It will go a long way in your completion of all things. Above all, listen to your body. When you feel fatigue, stop what you are doing and rest.

Yes, you still have plenty of time. Yes, you can still get out but in shorter increments so play your day wisely. Ask for help when you need it.

We have your best interests at hand. Take the time for yourself and each other. You both need it.

Council of 7"

*****

That same day brought Patty another quite astonishing meditation. Each of these seems more profound than the last.

"Three angels appear. I am lifted up and we go through the sky and out into the universe. I look behind me and see everything getting smaller.

There is gold light below and we move toward it. I wonder where the gates are located. They say, "For you there are no gates". We head toward a gold dome and land there. It looks like a city, only all gold. It is *the City of Gold*.

I have been here before but not like this. Everything glistens in gold. I see people, only they are just energy beings which emanate gold light. They can change to show a form like a person. I know this is only for my benefit. After they pass by I look back at them and they are only a gold glistening energy shape that moves. I feel so wonderful just to be in the presence of this energy.

The angels want me to know they merely accompany me here. I am here because I earned it. I have no shield of protection because I no longer need it. Wow, what a feeling!

It's time for me to leave here because I must attend class. We leave this beautiful place, my home. We cross over the boundaries. I can see the energy and colors as they change. The light is not as bright, the colors less vibrant. Ahead I see a large white building. They leave me outside of it.

Dad appears, grinning from ear to ear. "How was it?" All I could say was "Incredible!"

He opens the door and we go inside. I ask what this is all about. He says, "Just a class you need to take to continue your preparation". He walks me to the classroom and says he will see me afterward.

I walk into the room. It is full of others that are seated at desks. There are four empty seats. I take one in the middle of the front row.

A teacher comes in and says, "Welcome newbies! This is one of the last classes you have before your arrival. It will help you with the remaining time on earth. As your energy is transformed here, you have less energy there and you feel it. Some of you are up to 50%, others are anywhere from 20% on."

I ask about me and he says, "40%". He explains that either at night or in meditation they work to give us balance as we need it. He even drew mathematical equations on the board.

"Some of you will move quickly, others more slowly". I have just reached 40% and will be here for a while. It's necessary to complete what I started. The incidents I feel are to help me realize what is occurring. I feel other information flow into me but it can't be put into words.

Class ends and we leave. Dad is waiting in the hallway. He takes me to a kind of cafe. Mom is there sitting at a table. We sit down. They bring a bowl of something orange and yellow in color and like a thick syrup. He says, "You need to eat this".

I start to eat it. It has a mild sweet taste. "It's full of all the nutrients you need so eat all of it."

*****

Then, just two days later, the 22nd, Patty had another dream which again shows that she had nothing more to learn and that she is leaving.

"Ron and I are at college. I'm not taking any classes. He comes out of this office he was called to and we hug each other. He says, "Every time I come out of there I just want to cry".

"I know because I won't be there".

This dream is self-explanatory. Ron is the one taking classes, meaning he still has lessons to complete. The office is our place in the world. Hugging is the love we share, close to my heart.

*****

Another surprise came for Patty that same day in meditation. She was starting to realize just how much she learned to do in spirit world.

"The three angels are waiting for me. I move in the center of them. One is on each side of me and one behind me. I ask where we're going and am told, "Wait and see".

We move out into the universe. I can see stars in the shape of a horse (magnificent horse constellation). We move through the center of it and come out in a tropical setting. Beautiful trees are everywhere. I can hear birds singing.

There is a huge waterfall that cascades into a large pool of water. Dad is sitting beside the waterfall. I am to stand under it and then go into the pool. When I get out there is a white garment for me to wear. It has blue and gold trim down the front and is lined with jewels.

The angels are nearby. Dad says they will stay with me from here on out even when we are over there. "Why", I ask?

"It's necessary. They protect you from anything coming in to interfere".

Who Am I ...... Really?

"What happens now", I ask?

"We continue your preparation. We need you to get used to being over here more so today we will work on energy dynamics so you can practice more moving. I've brought some friends to help."

I see two of my aunts and a college friend sitting ahead at a table. Dad says, "Travel to meet them and we'll follow."

I take off, the angels are with me and Dad is behind me. It goes pretty well. I'm a bit off balance at first when I take off but I get it right back.

Dad says, "Now, use your thoughts to speak to them". I do in greeting them. Then I hear them all thinking at once. I can't understand anything!

Dad says, "Today we'll show you how to let their thoughts come in one at a time". He explains that instead of seeing them as a whole group, think of them as individual slots within a group. As you greet the group, focus on one at a time. I try it and it works. I hear them one at a time and they come in one right after the other.

Dad smiles and I know he's pleased that I could complete it on the first try. He tells me we'll work more on that later.

Then I ask about Robert. Ron had told me that in meditation he was told there is a Robert waiting for me over there. So, I asked. Dad says, "Yes he's waiting but you'll see him later. First, we have some more to experience."

We're standing in front of a tall white building. There are two others there I am to meet. Dad says, "They will work with you on your arrival. Their names are John and Stephen. They will help to shift any residual energy left over from your arrival and keep you in balance through your orientation. You are far above many due to your level and advancement. Basically, they'll just give you a tune-up."

I wonder what is next. Dad says, "Casey wants to see you". (Casey was a dear friend in Ohio that died unexpectedly some time ago.) I tell her I've missed her. We talk. She tells me it was so difficult when she left to let go of her boys. She knows they are doing okay. She's there for a while yet before she goes back in for another lifetime. She tells me we'll have plenty of time to catch up. She must leave now; her time is up.

Now I'm told its time to have some fun. Dad wants to show me something special. We take off and then we're in a magical place of thousands of butterflies! I've never seen so many butterflies! They are everywhere and even land on me. I hold out my hand and one lands in my palm. Its wings are the colors of the rainbow. Only now they talk to me and I hear them! It's so incredible! I feel like a child and I see Dad laughing. He says, 'There's so much more...." Then I start to zone out and they tell me to just let go. I can feel the physical me and the bed vibrating."

Chapter 29

For Patty and Ron, the changes continued. Sometimes they would be so subtle they really didn't notice. Other times, especially for Patty; it appears she was smacked in the face with reality.

Patty's next meditation occurred in January 24, 2012 and provided her with still more insight as to how to view past lives.

"During my prayer, I see Dad and the three angels waiting. An eagle comes and places his wing over me. I become one with his wing. Then I move up into his eyes. It is nothing I do, it just happens. He takes off and ends up landing on the picnic table in spirit world where Dad is waiting.

I want to ask some questions. Dad explains there is a timeline of our past lives. Each one is a slot on the timeline. To view them you only need to view the timeline, pick a slot and go into it. I try it and am immediately find one in Switzerland. I am a young woman; my father raises sheep. In a flash, I see another one that took place in Germany. The last one I glimpsed, I am a native in Africa. I completely zoned out the rest of the meditation".

*****

The meditations continue to offer more insight and education, sometimes leaving Patty's head spinning and her voice speechless.

Patty had a second meditation on that 24th that was so amazing and all as the result of merely focusing on a number.

"I am told to focus on #32. When I do, immediately I am in the middle of number 32. Jesus and I sit on a mountain top. He tells me the 32 paths of wisdom are like the spokes of a wheel.

Next, we appear in front of my house in spirit world. He raises his hand and my house disappears! It is as if it just crumbles in front of me. Then it is replaced by a huge beautiful castle. "This is what you've earned!" he says, "Create what you want after you get here. Now, I have a gift for you. Hold out your hand."

He gave me a diamond. It has a total of 144 facets, the number of a man who is of an angel. I am astounded and speechless to say the least. From here I zone out."

*****

What can you say after an experience like that? It was all so real Patty can't deny it anymore! Still she is in shock over what she has experienced.

Still, each day gave her with still so much more information to process. Her next meditation on January 26th, 2012 provided her with more instruction on energy flow and movement.

"Dad and a man with short white beard come for me. The angels are around me. Dad is carrying his briefcase. The man with the beard is an elder. He is here to give me a new level of teaching. It deals with what I experienced yesterday about movement.

There is a continuum in spirit world, all moving all the time. Movement creates and dissolves through thought and intention. Once can either stand still while things move or move with the flow of energy.

On earth, we can't see objects move that are solid and stationary. Yet they still are moving. Due to time and space we can't see them move. In spirit world, everything moves. The higher the realm, the more fluid the movement. One must be open to see the movement as well. All depends on thought. Ponder this. More will come later.

Dad tells me we need to attend a meeting. Then we're in a room with a conference table. There are seven beings there to ask me questions. Dad is there to help. I stand while everyone else is seated. It all happens in the blink of an eye and the next thing I know it is finished. They are pleased by whatever I said and I am congratulated. There is a menorah nearby and all the candles are lit.

After that we are outside a tall white building. It looks like a skyscraper. I feel very sick to my stomach. I ask, "What was all that about?"

Dad just said, "Last minute minor details". I feel as though I'm going to vomit.

I look down and I'm wearing a white robe with blue and gold jewels on the front. Dad tells me after what I experienced today, the book will be easier to write and flow quickly.

My energy continues to be adjusted which is why my stomach is so upset. He said to try meditating twice a day when I can and it will help ease the transfer. Again, I zone out.

*****

For Patty, this meditation was truly amazing. The fact that she is answering questions which are unknown to her conscious part, yet feeling the energy of it all in her physical stomach is mindboggling. She found is fascinating to experience, let alone try to explain it!

The next meditation on January 26th also had a profound impact. It made her realize we all have so many life experiences; yet we often have no idea of how we may have touched the lives of others.

"The three angels come for me along with a soul healer. She asks me to go with her. I am seated on my throne. She is standing beside me. I have on my gold crown and my gold robe. The church is full of people. "Who are they?" I ask. She explains these are some of the people you have helped in some of your lifetimes.

There are so many people. They file down the aisle toward me. From just looking into their eyes; I know how I helped them and I feel their love. I start to cry-so many, many people, men, women and children. There is so much love it's overwhelming!

The soul healer just looks at me and smiles. It is so inconceivable! They come from all walks of life and all periods of life. Their dress is from that particular lifetime. I am so honored and so humble. I feel very grateful to be in this presence. Mom, Dad and our relatives are all watching from the last row. They are so proud."

We leave here and the healer says, "Go with the angels; they have a surprise". They surround me and we begin to move. I am taken to the Angelic Realm. All that exists here are angels.

I am to appear before Archangel Michael. As I stand before him a gold and silver energy goes through me like a bolt of the purest, most incredible energy. It fills my entire being until I think I am about to explode! My arms fly up and my body starts to lift off the bed. I call out, tears flow down my face. A voice says, "*You have seen the glory through the eyes of God*"

I bow before him as I collapse. Then I am covered and surrounded by the angel's wings. No words can even begin to describe what I feel.

The angels take me back to the picnic table to meet Dad. He knew all about what I had just experienced. I can tell just seeing into his eyes. He just reaches out and hugs me. He holds me as I continue to cry. I am just so overwhelmed!

He brings me back and has me practice going in and out of my body and moving through the walls of the condo. What a difference! Now it is so easy for me, no balance issues at all. I am moving so fast Dad has to tell me to slow down." Wow! What a day! Patty never would have believed it if she hadn't experienced it!

*****

The last meditation for January occurred on the 29th. It brought in a whole new educational experience.

"I'm at a bus stop. A white and gold limo comes for me. Dad opens the door and I get in. I ask where we're going. Dad says, "There is another place we need to explore. It is called "*the City In-between*".

"In between what", I ask? "In between the levels", he says. 'It really is a level by itself'.

He goes on to explain. There are major levels of existence. Yet before a soul moves from one major level to another, they must experience the level of "In-between". Let's say a soul finished Level 1 and will go on to Level 2. He must first go to the level in-between to receive the needed preparation for exposure to Level 2. This preparation must occur before the transition to Level 2.

Within this place the soul receives information and exposure to the vibration of Level 2. It eases the actual transition.

Compare it to a child moving from one grade to the next in school. The first part of the new grade is spent reviewing the previous grade. Only then can the new grade information begin. So, that's where we're going.

In a blink, I see people moving about. There are small groups of people clustered together. I can tell they are in deep discussion.

Dad explains that first there are small groups. As each piece of needed information is realized, the class gets bigger. Then he shows me a graduating class ready to move on. Each is celebrated. I can see it's a big deal here and feel the pride in each person.

Dad says, 'The greater the level in vibration, the greater the experience of preparation. Only when a soul is ready can they transition to a new level."

*****

February began with more meditations. The meditation on February 2, 2012 left Patty far beyond being astonished. There are no words adequate to describe the experience.

"There is a white marble staircase leading upward. The steps are gold. I'm wearing a plain white dress. I start up the stairs and see Dad standing at the top. First, he's wearing a blue suit and red tie and then it changes to a tux with tails. When I reach the top step my dress changes to a beautiful white and gold wedding gown with a long train.

There are two gold doors ahead. I ask, "Where are we going?"

"This is your wedding coronation." he says. He holds out his arm for me to take. The doors open and he escorts me down a long aisle. The inside is like a beautiful cathedral. I hear harps and angelic voices; they are so beautiful it gives me goose bumps. The church is filled with people. They all rise as we enter. I see Mom in the front row with our relatives and she is all dressed up. There is an altar and on either side of it, twelve beings are seated.

I feel so honored to be here. Dad is so proud of me. "I've waited a long time for this!" he says. Tears stream down my face. We begin the walk down the aisle. The love I feel from Dad and all these people is extraordinary. Jesus is standing in front of the throne.

When we reach the end of the aisle, Dad helps me kneel in front of Jesus and then goes to sit with Mom in the front row. Jesus places his hands over my head. When he finishes he takes my hand and I get up. He places me on the throne. There is a jeweled crown on my head.

Now, we're at a special kind of reception. There is an orchestra playing beautiful music. The dance floor is empty. Dad bows and asks me to dance. We go out onto the floor. I feel so much love emanating from everyone.

"Your life as you know it will never be the same". We gracefully move all over the dance floor to a waltz. Being here, experiencing all this is something I never believed possible.

My whole body is numb. I zone out after that. When they bring me back, I can't move any part of my body. I am numb. I have to wait several minutes before I can move."

*****

So many changes take place there that Patty has a tough time coming back to the dense energy of everyday life.

Her meditation on February 8, 2012 began to show her once again leaving and saying goodbye to Ron.

"I am at a train station. A silver train pulls in and I get on it. Dad is waiting in the dining car. There are white linen table cloths covering the tables. Dad orders us some breakfast. He tells me he wants me to know this dining car has been moved from the back of the train to the front. Now it's right behind the engine. "Your feast begins here and will soon be realized", he says.

As I look outside when he said this, I see the rest of the train cars being uncoupled. I realize Ron is in the car right behind us on the train. There are ten others with him. The other cars slow down to a halt.

I stand on the back-porch area of the dining car. Ron is standing on the front porch of his car. We just look at each other and I can feel the strength of the love between us. From my car comes a white dove and from Ron's car comes a white dove. The two doves meet in the middle and merge together. We both wave and slowly turn around and go back into our separate cars.

As I sit down by Dad, he says, "Don't worry; a new engine will come pick them up". I see Enoch is the engine.

I realize this meditation is different because I can write and see all that is going on in the meditation at the same time. Something has been opened. I hear someone say, "It is the first seal that is open. There are six more to go."

The train pulls into the station and we get off. I'm not sure where we're going. Dad says, "First we'll stop and see your mom so your energy can be adjusted and you can release some as well".

I see Mom and we hug. She has me sit in a recliner chair and she hooks up and IV. Again, liquid gold energy flows through me. I thank her.

Now I'm inside a small room. Enoch is with me. Dad is outside. Enoch is sitting at a table. The recorder is across the table with my book open. From here I zone out."

*****

The meditation on February 9th, 2012 was brief in nature and yet Patty found the second seal was opened.

"I'm walking along the beach at the ocean. I see Dad walking toward me from the other direction. He takes my hand and we begin levitating and moving. A purple and gold mist surrounds us. We move through it and when we come out we're just above the picnic area.

He explains that I will begin to feel as if I don't have much energy to do things. It's part of the process. Some energy is transferred there and I still need enough energy to function in here.

Then Mom shows up and she's all dressed up. Next, I'm standing in front of my throne and wearing a gold crown. The top of my head is open and something is being taken out. My physical body, the right side of the top of my head is tingling all over.

I am kneeling in front of my throne with beings on either side of me. I hear, 'The 2nd seal has been opened." There is a gold ray of light flowing into my head.

Now we're back in Dad's office and I zone out."

*****

Patty's meditation on February 12th provided her with another opportunity of being free of limitations. Just being out in the universe and viewing the stars and constellations is very profound.

"Pegasus came for me. I am told to hold on tight, it would be bumpy at first. We had to get beyond the clutter. Once we break free of the barrier, it is smooth. There is a night sky like velvet with a million stars.

I see constellations shaped like a tiger and the big and little dippers.

Then I am in the picnic area. Dad meets me at the table. He says, "Today begins your last trial period. It will last three days. There is no preparation for it. You just experience it. Once completed, you will have met all the necessary requirements. It shall be sealed in one final meeting in the days to come. Our completion.

There are many here who have watched and benefited from your completion. We are very pleased with you both. You have earned your rest and reward. God's glory is yours".

*****

For Patty and Ron this month has been one of ups and downs. They were still riding the rollercoaster. Still on top of it is the fact the month of January Patty has felt pretty rotten.

She's had an ultrasound for an enlarged lymph node under her left armpit. But the diagnosis was enlarged lymph node that appears benign. Add to that some chest pains and severe burning and that's what has been happening. Yet any tests show nothing concrete.

She saw the doctor in mid-January and her blood pressure medicine was changed. But she still has trouble eating much and is often nauseous during the day. It seems as if her energy is more and more depleted.

Remember the bucket list? Well, Patty and Ron have been taking time to go through it one by one. One number on her list is lots of homemade ice cream. Now as nuts as that sounds... the place, which is only about a mile from their condo has the best ice cream they have ever tasted in their lives!! And just as women know, ice cream can cure many issues when you feel rotten.

But what Patty has come to realize is that whatever is on the bucket list really had no importance at all. Sure, it was all nice but what mattered the most was simply being with the man she shares her heart with and who loves her more than anything in the world and still having contact with her children. Still...they have their own lives to live.

Ron means the world to her and just loving him and sharing every moment... is more than enough.

Then two days later it was Valentine's Day. For Patty and Ron this was extra special this year. Ron surprised Patty with two dozen red roses, plus lots of candy and a card that is so beautiful she must share it.

"For My Wife, by your side is where I belong ...
Wherever life leads us, we'll go together.
Just being with you is all I ever really need to be happy.
I love you and the life we share and that's one thing that will never change.
        All of my love!
        Ron"

Add to that a beautiful dinner at their favorite restaurant and it was just a perfect day and the best Valentine's Day ever.

Chapter 30

March began with still more revelations. Patty's dream on March 5, 2012 again allowed her truth to come forward.

"Ron and I are hiking up a mountain. When we get to the top, we turn around to look at the view. Ron is standing behind me with his arms wrapped around my neck. It is such a beautiful view. The trees have all the leaves turned a beautiful mirage of autumn colors, gold, yellow, red and orange.

Then we hear someone coming from the other side of the mountain. Ron starts back down the mountain and says, "You stay and see who it is". Patty stayed there and saw a young man with blonde hair who is carrying a knapsack."

This dream is a guide coming from the other side for Patty. The knapsack shows there are things she needs to experience in spirit world. Autumn is the cycle of life. Something is about to end and something new will begin.

*****

The meditation Patty had on March 6, 2012 merely coincides with the dream.

"There is a huge cruise ship in front of me with a long gangway to get on. The ship is called the S. S. Celebration. Dad is at the top of the gangway. I start up to meet him. When I turn around and look, I see all the people I love on earth standing in a crowd. Ron is at the bottom of the gangway.

I'm halfway up the gangway when I turn around and run back to say goodbye. Ron holds his arms open and we embrace one more time. As

I kiss him, there are tears that begin to run down my cheeks. His eyes are filled with tears ready to burst.

Slowly we let go of each other and I turn and walk up the gangway where Dad is waiting. I see all my relatives and everyone I know in spirit world. They are all waiting for me. I get on the ship.

The crew begins to separate the ship from the gangway and the dock. When it is completely separated it is time to set sail.

Patty hears the engines revving up and the ship begins to move. She looks back one more time as she stands between her Mom and Dad.

Those on the dock wave goodbye and slowly the ship moves out into the open water. For Patty, it is a moment to be thankful for Ron, the love they shared and all they experienced in this lifetime together. From here a new life begins for each of them.

*****

So, the story continues ... for Patty, the beginning of March continued to bring additional information in her dreams and meditations.

From a physical viewpoint, she just hadn't been feeling well at all. She really had no energy and was nauseous often along with tightness in her chest. She still was only able to eat a small amount at a time.

Then her meditation of March 7, 2012 brought in a new source of information. 'I'm sitting by a stream and Dad and Enoch come toward me from the other direction. Enoch says, "Today is a day for you to celebrate. It is the physical opening of the 8th chakra. It is necessary as a means of travel during your transition. This process occurs a little bit at a time so your energy will be less disrupted than if it was all done at once.

The 8th chakra holds the divine wisdom of it all. Picture a gold vault and the door is encased in gold. Now picture the door open just a crack. This helps to understand the process.

That's why it is vital for the two of you to meditate each day. It helps facilitate the balancing of your energy.

Keep on working and you will be able to accomplish what is necessary. A great deal is going on around you, much of which we cannot tell you. We will speak to Ron in preparation of events to come.

You will find more difficulty as you return to your physical body. It is all a necessary part of the process. You will need to pace yourself in the regard as to having enough energy to accomplish things. Rest will replenish your field so listen to your body.

Your time is at hand so utilize all opportunities you can. All glory and honor is yours."

An eagle lands beside me to bring me back. He wraps his wings around me and we are gone."

*****

Now Patty did know there was an 8th chakra but she really didn't know anything about it. For many years Ron has had the ability to see into people's chakras and see a variety of things. He hadn't looked at Patty's chakras for years! It just hadn't occurred to them with everything else happening!

So, when she told him about the meditation, he said, 'Oh that is something we should have been doing a long time ago. That will give us more information"!

So, Ron began to look at her chakras. He could see where her first two chakras were closed off and the third was starting to close. The only time he had seen that before was when someone was going to die. As the upper chakras begin to open up, the lower chakras close down because they are no longer needed.

When he looked in her 8th chakra it was starting to open and was actually gold starting at the bottom. They decided to keep track at least once a week and see what changes took place.

As far as her dreams, it seemed she either slept so deep she didn't remember or maybe didn't want to remember?

Then her dream on March 11, 2012 manages to show her resistance to what was going on in that regard.

"I'm in a large house with a bunch of women. Guys would come after them to give them an injection and then have sex with them. Finally, Patty found ants so they'll check again. A very powerful man grabs her and she tries to resist but he still manages to give her an injection. She is amazed by what they are doing."

This dream points out these are all parts of Patty trying to merge while she keeps resisting. The reality is that you always want your aspects to merge! The ants relate to all the little things that annoy us.

Things seem to keep on moving and even Patty's meditation on March 11, 2012 seemed to indicate a bit of the work she would do once she got over to spirit world.

"I see a beautiful spiral staircase in front of me that leads upward. The steps are white marble and the railing is gold. Dad, Enoch and a group of people wait for me. The angels are there too. I know a few in the group but not most of them. I do see Enoch and Grey Fox.

Dad says, "This is the group you'll be working with." There are about twenty. Once I reach the top, we simply begin levitating. We end out in front of the creation building. Then we're in a conference room sitting at a large table. There are three of us that are new; the rest have been here awhile. Dad wants us to experience each other's energy. We each get up and share who we are.

Now I'm on an interstate highway driving around the curve of an exit. There is a pale-yellow Volkswagen coming straight at me head on. There is only one lane and nowhere for me to go. We merge together and then I zone out. (The Volkswagen was my car in high school)."

Even though Patty didn't know exactly what she'd be doing she at least met the people she'd work with in spirit world. Who would ever think that even over in spirit world you are employed!!

Patty's next pertinent dream on March 12th also proved to be quite interesting. "I'm taking the kids for a play date. I need four presents and I have three. I go back to the car and find the fourth toy. I wrap it and say to the woman, "This is creative wrapping".

This dream shows Patty that these are all her child aspects. She needs to relax and not take things so seriously. There is an important date she must keep. The gifts mean she is being acknowledged for her charitable deeds. The three deals with the trilogy and completion. She still has something left to finish or wrap up.

It began to seem as though each day provided just more confirmation and information about the upcoming events. For both Patty and Ron, it was quite astounding!

Her meditation on March 12, 2012 was extremely powerful! "I see both Mom and Dad are waiting for me. Dad says, "There are some things we need to go over". Then I find we are sitting in Dad's office. He's behind the desk and Mom is beside me. He looks at me and says, "Things are winding down. You need to finish your letters and anything else by the end of the week. You don't have much energy left. Use this week to tie up anything else, okay? There are others who wish to meet with you. The angels will take you this time."

The angels surround me and we begin moving. When we land it is a place of pure bliss. I am almost consumed by the joy I feel. There is a being in front of me that I see only as a pure gold energy without form. I am so humble in this presence. He welcomes me and says, "The time has come for one journey to end and for your final journey home to begin. We are all ready and waiting to receive you. All glory and honor is yours! Please allow yourself to let go now so we may further your preparation".

I zone out from here and what I feel is a heavy, heavy vibrating. It is mostly from the waist down and is heavier than anything I have ever felt before.

Also, today Ron again looked at my chakras. Today there is change in the 8th and even the 9th chakra is beginning to change.

So they are starting to see more changes on top of what Patty is feeling physically. Still she had no idea that on the next day, the 13th, not only would the blue lights appear again but the short dream she had would blow her away!

On March 13, 2012 Patty and Ron had gone to bed early because they were both worn out. They turned out the light and the television off about eight o'clock which was about normal for them. About eleven thirty, Patty briefly woke up to roll over and the blue lights appeared and asked for her to write.

"Hello once again. We thank you for this time and will try to be brief. We only want to touch base in regard to what has and will transpire from here on out.

First, you have completed what has been laid before you and surpassed our expectations; a job well done. We wish to reiterate what was said by those before us. Time is running down as far your time left so tie up any lose ends necessary. Share the time left as you can.

We honor you both. We realize the difficulty of this situation especially for Ron. There really are no goodbyes, only love shared between two souls. You shall continue to link together for an extended time in a way you would never believe possible.

The reality of all this is entering a new state of awareness in your conscious state. Realize times does not exist here. Only Universal Law and Divine Law have presence.

Ron will be cradled and held in the arms of comfort, I assure you. Grieve yes, but merely through the coils of the mortal shell. Celebrate yes, through all other avenues of existence. You will have your time together.

Your physical body will tell you the time frame that is left. Listen to what it says, there you will find your truth.

For those around you the shock will be immense but your words shall provide comfort. Again, we thank you for your commitment and perseverance. Your rewards will soon be realized.

Council of ALL"

*****

The next dream which also occurred on March 13, 2012 had such an impact on Patty that after having it, when she woke up afterward there was no way she could go back to sleep!

"Ron and I are at the hospital and seeing Dr. Johnson. She has all Patty's test results from the cardiologist. They are in front of us. She said, "There is a problem in the left atria, something or other, where there is a lot of backup in the heart being reabsorbed. Patty will need heart surgery."

"Tell me again what it is called", Patty said. Dr. Johnson replied, "I will just make you a copy".

The doctor's little girl, about three years old, is there riding on a tricycle and somehow the papers get wet. Dr. Johnson said, "Or I could dry these off." Then she says to her daughter, "Oh, you're going to meditate now? That's a good idea."

We're in the part of the hospital waiting for them to schedule the appointment and Dr. Johnson walks by and Patty says, "Do I go home the same day?" "Yes, they do something to regulate the heart."

Patty says to Ron, "they don't even keep you overnight." The doctor tells her that most people do well with it, except for one man who came back to the hospital.

This dream literally suggests how Patty will leave this earth plane. Of course, what it was revealing definitely stirred things up.

*****

Although Patty feels she has learned a great deal about the spirit world, she knows it is simply a drop in the bucket.

Her meditation on March 13th still left her feeling astounded. 'There is a kind of chute in front of me. I see a circular energy moving inside and it opens for me to step into it. When I do, the angels appear around it and I am shot up the chute. As I look behind me I see thick dense energy.

We land in the picnic area where Dad is waiting. He says, "The coordinates are 69 degrees and 39 degrees". I wonder what we're doing today. Dad tells me, "Actually more of your energy is over here. We must be careful what we utilize because we need to keep you in balance there. So, first we'll see you Mom for some juice".

I hug Mom and again I'm in a recliner with an IV of a gold liquid going into me. She brings me a bowl of something to eat. There is a large amount of it. It almost looks like honey but it sure doesn't taste like it. Yuk!

I wrinkle my nose and she laughs. It really tastes like a medicine someone tried to sweeten. "You must eat it all", she says. "It has vital nutrients you need for balance." I finish it and hand the bowl back to her. Actually, my insides do feel better. When I first got here I was sick to my stomach (physically).

"Enoch wants to see you", Dad says. We move to a stream and I see him moving toward us. He asks me to walk with him while Dad stays behind. We walk to an open area by the stream and sit down.

He moves his hand over the stream. I can see into it and see myself in the hospital. Ron is sitting beside the bed. Then an orderly in scrubs from the operating room comes in and Ron kisses me before I go.

I'm being wheeled down the hall to go into surgery. There is a sign above that says, "Surgery Pre-op". He pushes a button on the wall and two doors open. I am taken into the operating room and I can see them hooking me up to monitors and oxygen. An anesthesiologist sits at my head area. There are two nurses, one on each side of me and a third one over in the corner at a small desk. The nurse says, "They're going to give you something to relax and then the anesthesiologist will put you to sleep".

As I watch all this, it is as if I'm looking down through a hole from high above. Enoch waves his hand over the stream and the scene disappears. "That is enough for today", he says. "We'd like you to just let go and we'll work on you". I zone out again.

*****

Patty doesn't know what to think about everything she is able to see but she can't believe how real it is to go through the experience.

Angels have always been special to her; she even collected them for years. She had no idea just how profound it would be when she encountered them for real!

Her meditation on March 14, 2012 left her unforgettable images and experiences.

"There is a huge angel that comes for me. She is dressed in the most beautiful iridescent color. "My name is Anastasia", she says, and she is known as the Lady in Blue. She asks me to go with her. Then her large white wings wrap around me and I am totally encased in nothing but love! The softness of her feathers almost tickle!

I feel we are moving. I ask where we're going and she says, "Wait and see". I can feel us moving through the layers.

We go to land and she says, "We are at the Tribunal". "What is it?" I ask. She replies, "It is the final resting place of the soul memory of all who have completed their earthly journey. She explains that there is a final cleansing of the slate of the soul so to speak. Since all this energy is transformed karma, its cell memory is no longer needed.

We land before 24 light beings that only emit gold energy. As Anastasia lands and releases me, she bows before them in reverence.

Once again, this level of energy goes far beyond anything that I have experienced. They explain that any and all residual energy is being cleansed and released. Once completed, only the pure soul essence will exist.

Picture a classroom blackboard over years of use; even though the chalk is erased and the board regularly washed, there are still residual energy molecules there until it is replaced with a new blackboard.

This level of cleansing would provide you with the new clear level. It is merely the final sentiment of energy transformed.

From here you must guard your energy field, especially when present among the masses. It is vital to avoid any discord. I can feel this energy coming off me. It is the strangest feeling, as if my field is being vacuumed by feathers in an almost tickling sensation. They say it is to fortify my field. It feels as if I am encased in a gold energy.

Then this bubble gently pulls away from me. I see Anastasia once again and she wraps her wings around me and we start moving again. She lands and we are once again in the picnic area. I thank her for this incredible experience and see her begin to simply rise and move.

Dad is here smiling and says, "Congratulations! "You have just sealed the deal as they say. We are so happy for you. I know today is busy but can you just give me some time later? Okay, then we'll send you on through." I see a blue portal open up. Once inside, I am thrust through and return here."

*****

The next meditation Patty had on March 15, 2012, took her to another astounding encounter that left her speechless. "I'm standing at a bus stop. I look up and see Dad levitated above me. He comes down, takes my hand and says, 'Today we're going to do something different."

We begin to levitate up and four angels appear. We join hands in a circle and the entire circle begins moving. We pick up speed. I notice that there is the circle we created and then another circle of gold that surrounds the first circle. It is a thin band of gold. We move out into the universe and there are a million stars in the night sky. I can see a constellation shaped like a bird and we go into the center.

As we do, we burst forward as if we push through a time zone. We land at the picnic area. I start to wander and Dad says, "Stay with me here".

The next thing I see is a gold pyramid with an eye in the top. We go into it and I'm inside a huge gold dome. It is surrounded by stain glass windows that radiate all the colors of the rainbow; each putting off a shaft of light that goes to the center of the dome on the floor.

Dad tells me to land in the center of where the rays hit. I land in the center and it is as if a million bolts of energy flow through me from these shafts of colored lights. It is so powerful yet gentle at the same time. Dad says, "This is one of the Sacred Temples and you needed to have this experience".

We leave here and I find myself in Dad's office sitting across from him at his desk. I see one document on his desk. I wonder what it is. Dad says, "It's the last page so to speak". I can't read it. "After tomorrow you should have the rest of the material for your book, so let's leave this document for later. It's a bit too soon to sign it. "All these experiences are part of preparing you and adjusting your energy. Just be careful with it today".

Now it's time to go. He tells me there are so many waiting for your arrival, you wouldn't believe it! He takes me back to the picnic area and the portal opens and I go into it."

*****

After this meditation, Patty was more curious about what was in the document. The next meditation on March 16, continued from the day before with more insight.

"Once again Anastasia comes for me. She wraps me in her wings and off we go. Her wings are so soft. It is like being cradled in a cloud. What a wonderful feeling!

I can look down as we start to land. I see the picnic area and a large amount of people milling about. Dad and Father John are waiting for me. Suddenly I wonder why I only had one angel with me. Father John tells me it was all I needed.

Dad says, "Father John is going to explain some things but you won't be allowed to take them back with you. I'll show up when he's finished so relax and let go now".

I go and sit down at the picnic table and Father John is across from me. I don't remember anything else until we stand up when he's finished and shake hands. I also feel very sick to my stomach.

I see Dad wave to me and I walk over to him. I wonder what is going on today. Dad says, "Whatever happens today, just go with it, okay?" (I get the feeling he was also about to tell me something but then decided not to. Ok, now we can continue and we move up to Dad's office.

I see a document lying on the desk only this time it has a gold seal and is stamped *Final Document*. I ask if I can read it. Dad says, "Part of you knows what it says, but go ahead".

I begin to read, "This document contains the final transcription of one soul named Patricia Jean Stephens Plonski Kenner. It includes all earthly endeavors as well as all lifetimes experienced. The above-named soul has completed all necessary missions and numbers relating to soul comprehension and execution.

Who Am I ...... Really?

Therefore, this final declaration allows said above named soul to enter the gates of Heaven and the Realm of God the Almighty.

This decree is verified according to Universal and Divine Law and as such shall be scrutinized by no one. This soul essence has earned the place to exist for all eternity and is bound only by Divine Law and practice. Thus, shall we say this day of March 16, and the year two thousand and twelve in the time of earth years.

This soul is blessed by the Almighty Soul. So, say ye all"

Dad says, "We also will provide Ron with information". He turns the document around and I see the line for me to sign. He says, "You've earned this Princess, believe me, you've earned it."

I take the pen he hands me and sign it. As I write my name it appears in gold ink. Dad takes it and holds it in his hand. I say, "Please thank everyone here for all their help".

"You'll be able to do that yourself", he replies. "I think you've had enough for today".

He takes me back to the portal and hugs me. Then I go inside and as I do, I hear him say, "Tell Ron Happy Birthday!"

Chapter 31

Once again, this meditation allowed Patty and Ron to have new insight. They also realized that the meaning of whatever timeline they receive is not always what they think is to happen in here. Since everything must happen first in spirit world, there in can lie the discrepancy. They have learned that the best thing to do is to just allow the plan of the universe to unfold.

For the past few weeks or so, Patty keeps wondering how much more can be revealed. She has experienced so much and yet her instinct tells her that things are winding down. Her next meditation on March 17, 2012 seemed to indicate just that.

"Three angels come for me. They have a different vibration. It is gentle yet very powerful as in male energy. They surround me and off we go. We move out into the universe and again I see all the stars in the night sky. The sky seems like velvet.

Ahead I see a portal with purple swirling energy in a circle inside of it. We go into the portal and shoot out the end. We appear in a tropical setting. It's very lush with trees and flowers of all kinds. I hear a waterfall ahead of me and see Dad standing nearby. He says, "You must stand under the waterfall first. You really need a cleansing after yesterday".

I go into the falls and feel the water flowing over me. Being in the energy of yesterday for me now is like carrying a dead weight. I step out of it and feel exhilarated.

"Now go into the pool a bit". I do and the water is crystal clear and feels like bath water only energized.

I get out and notice a white gown is there for me to wear. "There are so many who wish to share your time, it's difficult to accomplish. But today, I'd just like to talk a bit." We head for a cluster of rocks nearby and sit down.

Dad says, "Neither of you realize just how enormous this project is and we understand why. The complexity goes far beyond your comprehension. We have shown you a great deal of what our real world is through both education and experience. You have far exceeded what we hoped to accomplish in our goals. These were pre-experiences to the event itself. There really is nothing left that needs to be shared, only the final event itself.

We have helped you prepare yourself so that others may learn from all you have experienced. It is not for those of weak mind, only those searching for truth. All souls must search for their own truth in their own time. Your words for some will be like an avalanche. For others, it is merely a seed which provides doubt in what they had believed. Each has its own merit. The code lies within the words.

We honor you both for your service. Be proud of all you have accomplished. Tie up any loose ends with the book for print and give thanks for all that has transpired. It has been a long road you have traveled. You have earned your rest.

Continue your meditations, it affords us the time for healing and balance. Simply we just prepare for your exit. That's all I have for now. Use the rest of the time to zone out so our preparation will continue. We all love you Princess!"

Dad"

*****

Somehow this meditation was a means of closing. She couldn't help wondering though, what her next meditation would provide. The next day, she was about to find out. Just when she thought it couldn't get any more overwhelming...

"I see a white marble staircase leading up in front of me. I look down and I'm wearing a white robe with a blue and gold sash in the front. The railing is gold on both sides. There is a purple mist at the top of the stairs and I start up them. Dad waits for me. I notice he has a suit on and is not carrying a briefcase.

I wonder what's up and he just smiles and says, "You'll see". I feel something is going on but have no idea what it is about.

"Today you'll move thorough another ceremony", he says. Meanwhile we had started moving with the angels around us. We stop in front of a huge white building that is iridescent. We go inside into a large auditorium. It is full of souls dressed exactly like me.

"Today you will receive your final commission into the White Brotherhood. You have always been part of it but this final commission is only for those souls who have completed and succeeded from the wheel of reincarnation".

We sit with others already seated. There is a stage in front of us. I see Enoch and 23 others on stage. They wear the same robe only their sashes contain colored jewels which differ, depending on their level of development.

We are called to the stage one by one and receive either a silver or gold staff or a gold crown. Each crown has various amounts of jewels. There are three staffs, either silver, gold or a combination of both. I wonder what I am to receive. Dad hears my thought and says, "You already have all the staffs".

I hear my name called and go up on the stage. I kneel before Enoch. He places a gold jeweled crown on my head. When he does, a very strong energy radiates through me. I hear Enoch's words as he places the crown on my head. "You are hereby receiving the final commission to the White Brotherhood in accordance with all Universal and Divine Laws". As I walk off the stage I feel a new presence of energy activated within my soul.

There are many seated here and we wait until all have been called forward. I notice only a handful of them have crowns, maybe five or six out of one hundred or so. I can see how proud Dad is, he's beaming! I am simply astonished!

When it's concluded we leave and find ourselves in a garden type of setting with the others. Special drinks are served. Dad tells me this particular nutrient activates some necessary soul energy that was placed into a dormant state during this last incarnation.

Just picture a part of your soul taking a long nap. Now it's time for that energy to wake up. This gives you one hundred percent of your soul energy. One only gains that through completion of all lifetimes and numbers of the matrix. It is the only way this reactivation can take place.

I am speechless. There are no words. I guess I'm wondering what it all means. Dad says, "From here on out you'll notice an enormous difference as far as your energy level and where it is or how much is available. You really are more over here with the least amount possible in there. So, be careful. It will make your actual exit much easier. We're ready and waiting. We all love you! I'll see you soon!

Dad"

*****

When the meditation ended I am so nauseous and feel as though there is a huge pressure in my head. It took a while for it all to subside.

Then the next day, March 19th, Patty had a dream that actually gave her a great deal of closure, along with explaining where she got the self-aspects she used to plan her life's blueprint.

"I'm in Pennsylvania in the small town where I grew up, with my brother and ex-husband. I go into a store to shop. I'm looking at shoes but I can't read the price on the ticket, even with my glasses. I run into Jasper (not his real name), my ex-fiancé from high school. He is with another man. At first, it's awkward. I am ready to hug him but know he doesn't want to hug me. We start talking and things lighten up. He lives in Wisconsin and is going back there.

I ask how his mom is and he says she passed on January 25th. I tell him my mom passed on May 17th. He shows me a memorial that's in the store. It's a large square white silk pillow that is on top of a display. You can turn it and on each side people have written something. He said, "You should write something from your mom to my mom". We both laugh and hug each other and I say, "Thank you so much for breaking up with me. It was the best thing you could have done!"

I tell him my brother lives in New Hampshire near the border. Then my brother, John (not his real name) walks in and I say, "John, you remember Jasper?" They shake hands. I tell Jasper that my oldest son, Christopher lives in Minnesota. If you need to stop on the way you could probably stay there overnight". I wake up."

*****

In this dream, the other man that is with my ex-fiancé is me. What ties all these male people together are the traits they have that I looked for in a man all my life. In the store shopping is trying to fill my needs and desires. Looking at new shoes is a life path that is unfamiliar to me. I can't see the value (price) I place on myself, my self-esteem. The moms are the nurturing aspects we all have inside of us. January deals with the loss of love and broken companionship (also the same month my fiancé broke our engagement). Number 25 is life graduating on all planes and evolving through opposite polarity.

May deals with prosperity and times of pleasure or may be seeking permission for something. The number seventeen is the soul in both worlds. Memorial is the need to confront the past, in order to move forward.

The states proved very interesting. Pennsylvania in numerology is number 53, Wisconsin is 43, New Hampshire is 67, and Minnesota is 38. You add the first and third state which equals 120, which is the total period of time in body. Wisconsin, 43 and Minnesota, 38 equals 81. 81 is 9 x 9 which is the individual's effort in the nirvana world realizing the act of pure love, the number describing the solidarity of excellence.

Number 43 is the influence of free will in a cycle. Number 38 is the impact of the individual in all this, assertion. The aspects of the male's strength, compassion and kindness.

For them, New Hampshire was a new beginning where everything opened up. So, Patty had used these male aspects as a means of what she looked for in a mate. Also, she never had closure on her broken engagement. This dream gave her closure. She also realized she was searching for these aspects and courage all her life. It was always there inside her, she just had to see it. Quite a dream to say the least!!

*****

Patty's meditation on March 19th again left her astonished and speechless! All of a sudden there were major changes.

"I see a purple and blue vortex of energy come for me and I step into it. When we land we are by a stream. The land along the stream has lush green grass. I hear the sounds of the birds. I look behind me and on the other side of the stream are all the people I love on earth. I'm walking forward by myself. Ahead I see a crowd of people. I know they are all in spirit world. As I reach them, they separate so I can walk into the center of them and they all move in around me. I am encased in their love. We begin to move forward as a group.

Ahead of me I see a large white marble slab that glistens white energy with gold twinkle energy in it. I see myself lying on this marble. It is as if I am asleep. I am wearing a beautiful white robe with a blue and gold sash on the front. The sash has many colored jewels. This is the part of my soul that has been asleep this whole time and I am told it is time to wake up that part of me.

Just as I reach the slab again the crowd separates. I see Mom standing at the head of it and Dad is at the foot. The crowd has all formed a circle around us. I lean over to wake up that part of me. When I do, she sits up and moves through me. As that happens, she moves to the other side and the part, which woke her up, turns around and just begins to become energy particles that dissolve. The rest of me, wearing the robe, moves forward between Mom and Dad. The three of us begin to move forward and the group follows behind us.

Dad explains that was I not finished with everything, that part would simply have continued back the way I came and then eventually crossed over to the other bank with those on earth. Only because I am finished and that energy is no longer needed was it allowed to dissolve.

We continue walking and I feel so exhilarated it's incredible!

Now we come to a place where mom, dad and I keep going and the crowd goes off in many directions to do whatever they must do. I simply send them my love and gratitude, while feeling their love in return.

Dad says, "Mom and I would just like to spend some time with you". We go to mom's house because she is still working to evolve to Dad's level. I see her house, it's simple but very nice. We go through beautiful French doors made of cherry wood out into a small lush courtyard filled with roses in so many colors. The aroma is like a fine perfume.

There is a beautiful dogwood tree in full bloom and a wonderful gardenia bush. A small table is set for four with a white linen table cloth and fine china. I see my grandmother sitting in the fourth seat and I go hug her hello. She kisses both my cheeks.

We all sit down to a small meal. Mom has done this all herself in my honor. It is her way of welcoming me. We join hands to pray and she squeezes my hand. When she does I look into her eyes and immediately feel her love so strong it brings tears rolling down my cheeks. I've missed her so much!!

It is time to leave and I thank Mom and hug her and my grandmother goodbye. Dad and I leave together.

I know we're not finished yet. We begin to levitate and move and immediately four male angels surround us and we move through the layers. Dad says, "I just want you to see your final creation before you go back".

We reach a level and it seems gold glistens everywhere. We are standing in the driveway of my house with the beautiful fountain which flows in the sound of music. Only this time what comes from the fountain seems to be a gold liquid instead of water. I look at my house and see gold rays that emanate out from the house. Dad smiles and says, "This is what you have earned and created. Congratulations, my dear Princess! Here is your palace".

From here I know it's time to leave and I know I will never be the same. Dad and the angels escort me to the border. Dad says, "Goodbye, I love you both". The angels bring me the rest of the way.

Who Am I ...... Really?

I am filled with so much joy and gratitude I could explode!!!

*****

All of these meditations and dreams have continued to evolve over the last few years for Patty, but up to this point they both still felt that they were some time away from the actual exit. That is until now . . .

It seems that everything is happening all at once as you see in the next meditation on March 20, 2012.

"Today as I begin my prayers to meditate, I immediately see an Anubis and another symbol of death. Anubis is holding a tablet. Then as I say The Lord's Prayer, I hear another voice over my voice which says, "Ye thought I walk through the valley of the shadow of death, I will fear no evil for thou art with me". I stop and start my prayer over again two more times. Each time I hear the same words again over my words.

When I finish the prayer, the Anubis is waiting for me. I see his tablet with names on it. Then I see a scene with four huge angels which surround me as I exit my body. I see Anubis off to the side. I rise up from my body and see these angels surround me as we move up. (I am observing this.) I see the silver cord is still attached and I watch as the slack is taken up, until the cord stretches and breaks free. They simply continue to rise.

The Anubis shows me the tablet. I can see seven names on it. I am listed as number six. I'm not sure what it means but I feel these souls are all collected the same day. These angels are still present and have a boundary of sorts around me while protecting me and I hear, "for the next three days". I feel very nauseous now.

From here I am taken to a cleansing area. It is a shower of sorts. I am standing under it naked. There is a silver liquid which flows over me to remove any residual dense energy. When I am finished there is a white gown with a blue and gold jeweled sash for me to wear.

I feel the angels still there and I see Dad coming toward me. He simply holds his arms out and I go into let him hold me. He simply holds me as the tears come. "I'll miss Ron so much!!!"

Dad explains that the link between us is so strong it will always be there, only transformed. For right now we both have healing to do. I understand and just send him my love so he will feel me.

Dad takes my hand and we walk. He says, "You need to feel the energy around you here. It is what heals you here, simply being in its presence. When you're ready, we'll go see the others waiting to celebrate your arrival. Just for now it will be us".

I see Mom coming toward me and I run to her. She hugs me and I sob from a place deep within my soul. Finally, I stop.

It is so beautiful and peaceful here. It is as if the beauty of the energy absorbs my tears. Dad says, "You needed to experience this because we're getting very close to the end of the chapter. There is not much time left. You both are ready whether you realize it or not. I think this is enough for today. The rest will come later."

They both hug me and the angels lift me and slowly bring me back into my body.

*****

Coming out of this meditation, Patty thought her tears would never stop. During the meditation, she felt as if part of her heart had been torn out. Her love for Ron is so very strong.

After all these months, after all this meditating and journaling and after all this writing, things really seem to be happening. She wondered if either one of them was really ready.

Patty found herself going back over the letter which Ron had given her on Valentine's Day, February 14, 2012. This letter meant everything in the world to her.

"Dearest Patty,

Today we celebrate our love and the devotion we have for each other. I can say without any hesitation that you are and always will be the love of this life and many more to come. You impressed me the very first day I met you and you haven't stopped.

This journey with you has been greater than anything I could have created or imagined. We did it together. Every step of the way there were four feet walking in the same direction.

When we first came together I was afraid of what lay ahead for us. Now I realize my fear was nothing. You have been the inspiration for this soul more times than you will ever know.

You and only you are the one thing in this world that I truly cherish. Any thought of not being with you cripples my soul from grief.

You are the one thing I did right in this world. You are amazing to me and you always have been.

I am a better man and human being having been on the receiving end of your love.

No matter how much space is placed between us, I will always live in you and you in me, and that's the way it will always be.

I love you unconditionally my love. You are the candle that gave light so I could have hope and promise. You truly reign the heart that God gave you.

I will love you beyond the stars.

Ron"

For Patty, the questions remained... where was this going? Was she really leaving and when?? Everything she experienced over the years told her yes, but her heart... that was another story.

www.ingramcontent.com/pod-product-compliance
Lightning Source LLC
Chambersburg PA
CBHW021124300426
44113CB00006B/284